ADVEN1

IN COAL:

The beginnings of the coal mining firm of

HENRY BRIGGS SON & Co.

in Yorkshire c1826 to 1890

by

JOHN GOODCHILD, M.Univ.

A
MONOGRAPH
OF THE
NORTHERN MINE RESEARCH SOCIETY
AUGUST 2000

For the congregation of the Westgate Chapel (Unitarian), Wakefield,
the spiritual home of Henry Briggs and his two sons
and of the author of this book.

ISSN 0308 2199

ISBN 0 901450 53 7

Typeset in 10 point Times New Roman

by

N.M.R.S. Publications.

PRINTED

by

FRETWELL
PRINT AND DESIGN

Healey Works,
Goulbourne Street, Keighley,
Yorkshire, BD21 1PZ

for the publishers

THE NORTHERN MINE RESEARCH SOCIETY
KEIGHLEY, U.K.

Cover illustration:
Sketches of Silkstone Pit at Whitwood.

CONTENTS

FIGURES

PLATES

INTRODUCTION

The rich documentation of the complex of collieries operated by Henry Briggs and his successors allows posterity to see something more than is usual of a wide variety of the concern's story and associations. The owners, their personal and business interests; the pre-history of the business back into the 18th century; methods of financing new developments; the provision of the necessary housing and social ancillaries; the growth of the coal markets by waterway, rail and steamer; the use of small coal in brickworks, chemical manufacture and gasworks; mining methods, and the early use of coal-cutting machinery, together with conditions of work for the collier; and the radical social experiment with profit-sharing and a worker-director are some aspects of the story of this major colliery which can be examined through the papers, plans, maps and photographs which have survived, and which are explored here up to the 1880s.

BEGINNINGS IN COAL

Henry Briggs was born at Ward's End in the township of Halifax in August 1797. He was the third and youngest son (of six children) of the first marriage of Rawdon Briggs of Halifax (1758-1835), a Hull man who was an incomer to Halifax and who was in the woollen industry before becoming prominent in local banking affairs, in which latter business he was succeeded by his two elder sons. Henry's mother, who died just before he was five, was a member of the Currer family of Skipton, and his father was a partner in the firm of Currer, Briggs & Co. of Luddenden Foot near Halifax, woollen yarn and carpet manufacturers, which firm Henry joined in 1816.

Henry Briggs married in June 1824. His wife was Marianne, the younger daughter and co-heiress of the colliery owner James Milnes of Flockton Manor House near Wakefield, who had died in 1803. Briggs continued to live at Blackwood in Sowerby near Halifax, however, until about 1825, when he removed to Overton Lodge, close to his wife's mother and family at Flockton Manor House.[1] In 1815 his wife's elder sister Margaret had married William Stansfeld, one of whose own brothers had married Henry Briggs's

PLATE I Henry Briggs and his wife Marianne (née Milnes).

sister. Like the Briggses, the Stansfelds were Unitarians. Three of the Stansfeld brothers of Leeds, Thomas Wolrich (1779-1853), Henry (1795-1829) and Hamer (1797-1865), were by April 1823 partners with Henry Briggs in the firm of Stansfeld, Briggs & Stansfeld, cloth merchants of Leeds. The firm at that time wanted to establish an agency in London in lieu of doing their business through various dealers there. Mr Stansfeld was quoted as saying that his brothers and Mr Briggs were wealthy men, very prudent in business, while William Aldam senior, another Leeds cloth merchant, when asked for his opinion in confidence, described the Stansfeld partners as of "*an old & respectable family in Leeds ... Briggs their partner was lately taken in being the son of a Banker at Halifax of great respectability*". Some doubts were, however, cast upon the capacity of the capital available to the firm which also had a branch, as Stansfeld, Briggs and Carbott, in Hamburg in relation to the business done, and the difficulties of the mid-1820s led to the firm's collapse, a commission in bankruptcy being issued against the partnership in April 1826. In his will Henry Briggs alluded to this collapse as "*one of the most painful circumstances of my life*", although he was able to weather the storm with a payment of £2635 19s 4d from the marriage settlement - to which incidentally he had brought nothing himself - and in 1828 his own two brothers, the bankers, bought back his interest in the marriage settlement property for £1500 from the assignees. Mrs Briggs's portion had been worth some £12,000.

In April 1823, over a year before his marriage, Henry Briggs had been described as being the owner of a colliery near Halifax which was worth nearly £6000, but of this concern nothing is known, although the experience provided by its management would no doubt be useful in later years. Subsequent to his firm's bankruptcy, Briggs removed to live at Overton Lodge to take an active part in the colliery business which had for some years been run as Milnes & Stansfeld and to which he had himself been admitted as a partner in the month before his marriage.

There must have been considerable perturbation in the families at Flockton Manor House and at Blackwood when, in the year following Henry Briggs's marriage, his wife's eccentric and ageing uncle, Richard Milnes junior, then living at the gaunt but handsome (and still standing) Netherton Hall, published his autobiographical and miscellaneous book, "*The Warning Voice of a Hermit Abroad, who has been compelled to write in his justification, and he hopes for the good of mankind, under the protecting hand of Divine Providence, (for which he can never be thankful enough), through a long and tedious passage, of the most Imminent Perils and Dangers of being extinguished, and sent to his grave*", in 1825. Apart from the breathless length of its title, the work was curious in a number of respects, the one which most concerned the family being the section of the autobiographical portion of the compilation which castigates James Milnes and his wife, the new Mrs Briggs's father and mother. Old Richard Milnes died at Netherton Hall only a few years later, in 1832, at the age of eighty one. His book had outlined something of how the Milnes family had come to be engaged in coalmining and something of how the new Mrs Briggs's father had come to take over the colliery's ownership and running from his brothers, in dubious circumstances. The story is augmented from original sources and in outline is as follows.

Flockton Colliery, into whose part ownership Henry Briggs had come, was already of some antiquity and size. It opened between 1772 and 1775, at a cost of some £6000, and coals were being sold from it in the latter year by Richard Milnes of Flockton, who was a farmer, maltster and timber merchant, and his four sons. It had also been linked to the navigable River Calder at Horbury Bridge by a wooden waggonway. The colliery was one of the first large ones in the upper Calder valley and pits from it were also opened in Shitlington township. Its promoters took early advantage of the juxtaposition of good quality coals, cheap water transport and expanding markets. Richard Milnes senior died in 1779, and from the 1780s the colliery was managed by his son James Milnes alone, his brothers being paid £300 a year each as rent. He died in 1803 and the colliery was apparently subsequently managed by his widow. In 1814 the gross value of the business, including a furnace which had been opened at Emroyd, amounted to £39,629 6s 6½d. Old Mrs Milnes lived on until 1858, when she died at the age of eighty-nine. Her daughter Marianne Briggs lived to the age of eighty-five.

Henry Briggs was still very actively concerned in the management of the Flockton and Emroyd collieries, run as Stansfeld & Briggs, as the new Newton and Whitwood collieries were being developed from 1836 and 1840 respectively. The early death of his friend, partner and brother-in-law, William Stansfeld, in June 1836 presumably placed a large additional burden upon him, as his eldest nephew was then just over 27, though old Mrs Milnes and her daughter, Mrs Stansfeld, were highly capable women who had a long experience of running a coal mining business. Only a few, although curious, references to Briggs occur in the manuscript history of the Denby Grange Colliery written by Lady Lister Kaye. For example, in 1840, Stansfeld & Briggs successfully tendered for the supply of coke to fuel the locomotives of the Manchester & Leeds Railway, making the coke at their Emroyd Colliery. This was initially a highly lucrative trade, and the contract yielded 14s 8d per ton supplied. Briggs was said to have made subsequently *"every effort to obstruct"* the adjoining colliery owner, Sir J.L.L. Kaye, Bt, when he proposed to enter the coke supply market at what was hoped would be 13 shillings a ton. The Lister Kaye coke ovens were opened in March 1841 and both the Lister Kayes and Stansfeld & Briggs - the latter in renewing their contract - had to be satisfied with 12 shillings a ton. Lady Lister Kaye also mentions the strike of Stansfeld & Briggs' colliers in October 1841 following an underground explosion there, and the visit to their collieries by a gang of Plug Rioters during August 1842:

"The Mob visited Mr Briggs' Works and tapped all his boilers and Water Engines as so effectually to stop the works, and were aided in these lawless acts by his own Colliers."

although the matter seems not to be reported in the Wakefield newspapers. There were also major difficulties during 1842 and 1843 with trades unionists. This was indeed a busy and challenging period for Henry Briggs, with his responsibilities spread over the three groups of collieries. It had been one also up to June 1840 when he had also been *Chairman of the Coal & Iron Masters' Association*" - an organisation which seems to have crumpled in the very difficult period which followed his leaving its chair.

During the 1840s, however, Briggs had sufficient energy to continue to take an active part in the affairs of the West Riding Geological & Polytechnic Society, on whose Council he sat, and in the affairs of the new Wakefield Farmers' Club, to whom he read at least one (published) paper. Presumably the burden of the Flockton and Emroyd collieries was lessening, as his nephew James Milnes Stansfeld, born in February 1816, helped with the running of that business, ultimately taking it over entirely, but already taking a part in its management by 1841.

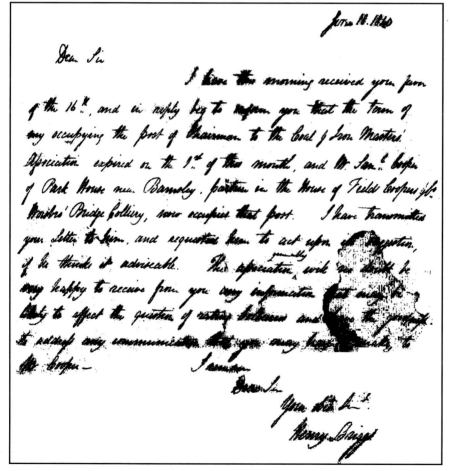

Fig.1 Letter from Henry Briggs, 1840.

In February 1849, "*A Coal Proprietor*", presumably Briggs, wrote in *The Leeds Mercury* of the contrast between the methods of working the coal at Barnsley and that at Flockton and Whitwood. The latter method was claimed to be much less liable to take human life in the event of an explosion. In Barnsley, the coal was worked outwards in panels from the main roadway, so that the men and boys were further from the main roads the more the panel's coal was worked, while at Flockton and Whitwood the coal was worked from the ends of the two side roads, back towards the main road.

There were obviously ample opportunities for Henry Briggs to become aware of the advantages of working the deeper seams in the eastern part of the exposed coalfield which were made available for commercial exploitation for the first time through the authorisation of a "*cross*" of steam-powered railways, which were all authorised by Acts of 1836 and which all happened, by topographical chance, to meet at or close to Normanton. How Briggs's attention was drawn to the matter can be no more than surmise, bearing in mind that in 1840 he was chairman of the local "*Coal & Iron Masters Association*", an active member of the local Geological Society, acquainted with the locality through his slightly earlier activities at Newton near Castleford, and a partner with Charles Morton who had for some time been manager at Newmarket Colliery, just across the river. The first Briggs' colliery in the locality was out of reach of the new railway network, with the railway in the vicinity being cut off from Newton by the navigable river Aire, the York and North Midland line lying to the south of the river and Newton to the north. A lease of the so-called Upper and Lower seams was taken in December 1836 from T.D. Bland of Kippax Park by Henry Briggs and his sister-in-law (who had become a widow in June that year), for 21 years, but these seams proved to be unremunerative, and the sinking was continued to the lower Warren House Seam, at 142 yards. The colliery is shown on the one inch Ordnance Survey, surveyed in 1838-40, as "*Newton Colliery*" and had a half a mile long tramroad down to the Navigation in the Aire. Adam Jessop, the first Castleford surgeon (he was known complimentarily as Dr Jessop), records accounts against Stansfeld and Briggs of Newton Colliery in 1841 to 1846, inclusive. Perhaps the major point of significance of Newton Colliery is that it was the first successful sinking in the West Riding through the Magnesian limestone to the coal beneath. The colliery continued at work until the expiry of the lease in 1857, after which it was continued as Henry Briggs and Son. The partners had built colliers' cottages in this very rural spot, together with a chapel, and the lessor had built cottages too. Some of the cottages survived until the demolition of the last row in the mid 1960s. In 1863, as the Briggs' interests became more concentrated on developments in the Normanton and Methley area, the colliery at Newton was sold for £9000 to H.K. Spark, the Briggs' erstwhile partner, and their interest in Newton ceased. Spark took the Newton coal at minimum rent of £600 (£120 per acre) for 21 years from 1863, and he continued to work it until official abandonment in 1880. In 1868 Spark was sinking to deeper seams with a shaft which William Aldam,

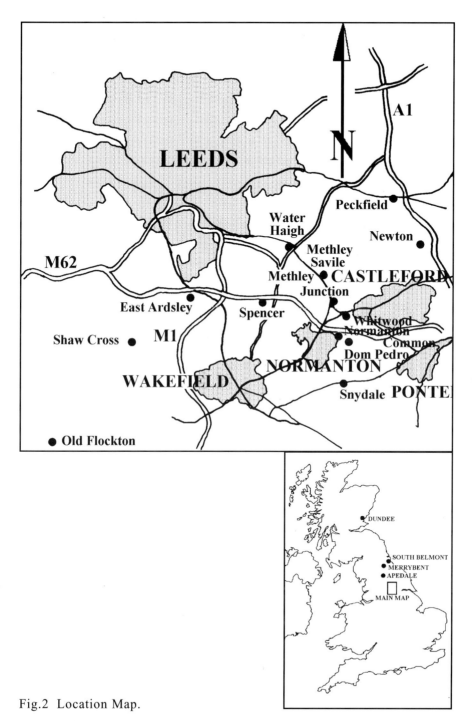

Fig.2 Location Map.

11

the Chairman of the Navigation, described in his personal notebooks as being *"as large as any in the district"*. It was proposed to sink to four or five virgin seams and to have a basin for coal-loading into barges. After Spark's time, in 1876, ninety two of his miners prosecuted their employer J.H. Garbutt for non-payment of their wages; the manager claimed he could not get in touch with Garbutt.

A new Briggs' colliery, which was to prove infinitely more important and whose lineal descendant was to continue working far into the era of coal nationalisation, was that at Whitwood. Here, Henry Briggs had no backing from his relatives, but took Charles Morton as partner. The pair took a lease of the Shale and Stanley Main seams under the Earl of Mexborough's estate at Whitwood, a township centred on the tiny agricultural village of the same name, whose whole population in 1841 amounted to only 417, including the population of the industrialised (with pottery and glass works) eastern extremity which was a suburb of the industrial village of Castleford. The 21 year lease, signed in December 1841, was to operate from the October of the previous year, that presumably being the date on which coal was first proved. The area leased was some 404½ acres under old enclosures and some 181½ under recently enclosed land. Both the area and the period of the lease were substantial, and two seams were taken, the Shale Coal and the (Stanley) Main Coal, together with such parts of the seam lying twenty yards above the Shale Coal as the partners, Briggs and Morton, desired to work. The rents payable, from the second year of the lease, were:

2nd year minimum	£540	for	3 acres
3rd	700		4
4-7	900		5
8-21	1200		5

There was also £70 per acre to pay for the Shale Coal and £110 per acre for the Stanley Main above the minimum, rising between the 8th and the 14th years to £80 and £130 and subsequently to £95 and £145 respectively.

Powers were granted to make coke and to burn bricks and lime, and, with Mexborough's approval, to build railways to the nearby York & North Midland Railway and to the Aire & Calder Navigation, but not to carry non-Mexborough coal upon them. The partners had already built twelve cottages, and the Earl was to allow the capital cost of these, charging 6½ per cent to the partners.

Coal had in fact been worked in Whitwood township at a much earlier date, making it similar to many other West Riding townships where coal began to be worked on an altogether larger scale from the period of development of much larger coal markets, largely created by the railways, in the mid 19th century. In the case of Whitwood, a shaft is shown close to the ancient earthwork known as Fairies Hill on a plan of 1752, and another existed close by. The new Briggs and Morton colliery at Whitwood lay between the York and North Midland Railway and the Aire and Calder Navigation's branch in the Calder itself, although for a short initial period there may have been only a connection with the former. The sites of the two first shafts have recently been cleared of their superincumbent coal slack and duly filled and fenced. In 1843 "*Dr*" Jessop of Castleford provided medical services which he charged to the account of Briggs and Morton, Whitwood Colliery.

Charles Morton, Henry Briggs' first partner in the Whitwood Colliery, was a man of both worth and parts. Born in Sheffield in October 1811, Morton was a son of the collector of rates for, and agent to, the Overseers of the Poor of that town. He was educated at one of the best known schools in Sheffield, that run by the Reverend Peter Wright, the Unitarian minister at Stannington, first in the vestry of the Upper Chapel and later at Portobello. At the age of 13 he had been apprenticed to J.T. Leather, C.E., of Sheffield, the designer of, among many other works, the ill-fated Bradfield Dams. After some time with Leather, during which he was taught surveying, levelling and "*planning*", Morton was sent to learn specifically the colliery trade with a Mr Stobart who was the Earl of Durham's colliery agent at Chester-le-Street. On completion of his apprenticeship, he was sent to Edinburgh University, where he is said to have taken "*honours in chemistry and geology and in mathematics*". Being by this time duly qualified, Morton returned to his home town and for some time acted as agent at the Thorncliffe Ironworks and for a colliery near Rotherham which belonged to members of the same firm. His professional standing was such as to allow him to be called as an expert witness before Parliamentary committees on several local Bills. During this period, Morton became well known in the cultural life of Sheffield, taking a principal part in the establishment of the Mechanics' Institute there and delivering lectures to audiences of working men. One local poet was indeed moved to verse upon hearing one of Morton's lectures, but others considered that the results of recent geological researches tended against religion and on one occasion Morton and a fellow lecturer were pelted with rotten eggs.

In 1835 Morton's father died, and for a while Charles continued to perform his father's duties as collector of the poor rates, but in February 1837 he left Sheffield on being appointed "*Colliery Agent*" or manager for Messrs J. & J. Charlesworth, a rapidly expanding firm of colliery masters which soon became the largest producers of coal in Yorkshire. Charles brought his mother and a younger brother with him to the Wakefield district, but only remained with Charlesworths for two years. He then decided to enter private practice as a land and mineral surveyor and colliery agent at Wakefield, in a period which was witnessing a very considerable expansion in that industry and neighbourhood. For a short time he was also manager for Thomas Wilson's new and ill-fated Darton Colliery, probably on a part-time basis, but in 1840 he entered into partnership with Henry Briggs in taking leases of coal at Whitwood, adjoining the newly-opened York and North Midland

Railway. By 1841 Morton was living at Normanton, presumably to manage the colliery, although he is not mentioned in the Normanton rate survey of 1844.

Educated by a Unitarian minister, Morton, like Briggs, was an active Unitarian in adult life, and he was appointed a Trustee of Westgate Chapel in Wakefield in 1838, along with Briggs. He paid chapel pew rent from 1839 and, like Briggs, he was one of the Trustees who opposed the Reverend John Cameron, the Chartist, out-spoken and Scottish minister, in the mid-1840s. Morton ceased to pay pew rent after 1844, but returned in 1851 and continued at the chapel until he left Wakefield after his breakdown in 1868. With Briggs, he had been a founder-member of the West Riding Geological and Polytechnic Society in 1837.

Morton seems to have left his partnership with Briggs in 1846, as he is referred to as a coal master in the Wakefield Mechanics' Institution membership books in 1841-46 inclusive. He then possibly became a partner with Henry Holt of Wakefield, land and mineral surveyor, for some time. He was also a member of the Wakefield Committee for the support of the Great Exhibition, and he proposed a site for a market in the town before a Parliamentary Committee.

"An Act for the Inspection of Coal Mines in Great Britain" (13 & 14 V., c.100) was passed in 1850, following the report of a Parliamentary Committee, and in November that year Earl Fitzwilliam, the South Yorkshire land and mineral owner and coal master and an hereditary Whig, nominated Morton to be one of the four first Inspectors appointed by Lord John Russell's Whig Government. Morton was appointed, but the fact that he was also a moderate Liberal was probably coincidental.

By this time, Morton had long experience in the coal industry in a variety of capacities and was well known and respected within the northern part of the extensive area of his Inspectorate, which included Yorkshire, Derbyshire, Nottinghamshire, Leicestershire and Warwickshire. His primary task was to reduce the various hazards endemic to the industry by persuading both coal masters and colliers to improve their safety standards. The means by which Morton induced the coal masters, and particularly the smaller masters whose net profits allowed them little to spend on maintenance and safety, to be increasingly aware of their responsibilities in this direction, are of obvious interest, especially when considered in relation to the overall technical and economic development of the industry in the mid-19th century.

Morton attacked the problem from a number of directions, and his first printed Report, covering seven months of his work, illustrates his original *modus operandi* - although his methods naturally altered as successive Parliamentary enactments gave the Inspectors stronger coercive powers.

During this period, Morton seems to have retained some interest in the Whitwood Colliery and continued to act as a mining consultant, but upon the passing of the second Mines Inspection Act in 1855 (18 - 19 V., c108) the position of Inspector became important enough to occupy its holder full-time. In 1866, having held the office of Inspector for some 16 years, and being then in receipt of the handsome salary of £800 a year, Morton resigned at the age of fifty-five as a result of stress over the Oaks Colliery disaster of that year. He lived in retirement until November 3rd 1881 when he died at Southport at the age of seventy-one.

PLATE II Henry Currer Briggs.

In 1851 Henry Briggs took the tenancy of Outwood Hall, a large Gothicised mansion of c1816 on the northern outskirts of Wakefield. Two years later, he leased the mansion and its parkland for 21 years at £160   7s   0d per annum, and used the premises as both home and office until his death. His son, Harry Briggs, also lived at Outwood Hall after his marriage, but, after Henry Briggs's death, Harry Briggs and his family moved away and the remaining Briggs' fixtures and furniture at Outwood Hall were sold to the incomiong tenant, Mr Langhorne, who was the Probate Court Registrar at Wakefield, in the middle of 1869. The house has long been demolished, but the stable block, in an architectural style similar to that of the house and bearing the date 1816, survives.

One of Henry Briggs' particular interests was in agriculture. In 1843 he read a paper, which was published, on the subject of growing wheat or other crops successively on the same land, to the Wakefield Farmers' Club, and he became that society's honorary secretary until his resignation in May 1851. He was an early member of the Yorkshire Agricultural Society, founded in 1837, and a member of its Council from 1848 to 1854. His grandon wrote that he *"always farmed a great deal of land, in conjunction with his collieries"*. He was also a promoter and subscriber to the West Riding Steam Ploughing, Cultivating & Thrashing Co. Ltd, formed in 1862 to provide steam tackle for hire, and he was among its largest subscribers and as well as being one of its directors.

When the Yorkshire Geological & Polytechnic Society was founded at Wakefield in 1837, Briggs was again a founding member and in this instance a very active one, taking a major role in the establishment of the society. For a long time he was a member of its Council. He also presented several papers, occasionally chaired meetings and was the local secretary for the Wakefield district. The Society played a vital part in the success of local coal mining ventures, and in developments into deeper strata and below the eastern Magnesian limestone, through its promotion of a greater and more detailed understanding of coalmining geology, and many of the larger coalmasters were among its active members. Its story is told in detail in J.W. Davis's *Golden Jubilee History* of 1889, together with details of Briggs's concern with it.

Briggs also took a leading part in the affairs of what was probably a newly-established coalmasters' association, which apparently covered the whole of the West Riding coalfield, as its chairmen came from both the West and South Yorkshire sections of the coalfield. Briggs was its chairman in 1839 and to June 1840, when he was succeeded by Samuel Cooper, the iron and coal master of Worsborough Dale.

Henry Briggs was brought up as a member of the English Presbyterian (by his time theologically Unitarian) congregation at Northgate End Chapel, Halifax, and he adhered to rational dissent throughout his life, marrying into it in June 1824 at Thornhill Church, the parish church for the townships of both Flockton and Shitlington. The marriage was conducted by the Rev. Edward Ridsdale, a near relative of Mrs Briggs, as Nonconformist marriages - except for Quakers and for Jews - were not allowed until 1837. Henry Briggs began to attend Westgate Chapel at Wakefield, to which Mrs Milnes and her daughters had become attached, presumably through the marriage of a niece of Mrs Milnes to Thomas Johnstone, the minister of that Chapel. James Milnes, who died in 1803, appears never to have been a Unitarian, but his family were paying pew rents there by 1834 as Stansfeld & Briggs, and this business pew-rent paying continued until 1851 with the rents including sittings for servants. Individual members of the Briggs family continued to pay pew rents into the 1880s, and D.H. Currer Briggs remained a trustee of Westgate Chapel until the 1960s. In 1841 the clothing made at the colliery school of Stansfeld & Briggs at Flockton was sent to a Unitarian Mission in London, and, later in the 1840s, Briggs employed a man called Yelland (assumed to be the Robert Yelland who, from 1856 to 1859, was successively Unitarian minister at Billingshurst, Ringwood and Sidmouth) as schoolmaster and Unitarian missionary at Overton. By September 1847 Yelland was described as employed by Briggs, and in 1850 he undertook mission work for the West Riding (Unitarian) ministers' meeting, although only until the end of September.

At Flockton, the Stansfeld and Briggs families ran a social system which was acclaimed by the government reporter of 1841. He claimed that:-

"The Flockton system has given the flattest practical contradiction to the asserted inaccessibility of the poor to kindly and civilizing influences; and equally so to the doctrine that refinement and labour are incompatible."

A Sunday School had been run since about 1803, the date of old James Milnes's death, in a room which was ultimately found inadequate and replaced by a purpose-built one, 56 feet long and with an ante-room, and connected to the Milnes and Stansfeld's own mansion, the Manor House. The walls were covered with pictures and a piano was provided, and the children attended here each Sunday morning and/or afternoon, before attending the services at the village church. In the Sunday School, reading and spelling were taught and tickets for attendance issued (allowing for the acquisition of bibles, prayer books and hymn books), and there was an annual examination cum social event, with parents present.

On Monday afternoons, the schoolroom was opened for more advanced teaching, and both boys and girls were taught reading, writing, arithmetic, geography, grammar, dictation, lessons from subjects (sic), drawing and composition. The girls were also taught sewing and marking for clothes making. The village had a library, a savings club, and a provident society for parents. On Wednesday evenings, a singing class with some 28 older boys and girls met, and undertook some serious singing. For at least three months in 1841, *"a school of mutual instruction for men"* was held on Thursday evenings and supplied periodicals, chess boards and dominoes for a small subscription. There was also a Temperance Society and a Sunday class for older boys.

"A large and beautifully situated gymnasium, or playground", open to all, was open on Tuesday and Saturday evenings. It had a gravelled walk for the elderly and was used for games, gymnastics and cricket. Allotments were provided, too, and a Cottagers' Horticultural Society formed. In all these concerns - and it might be mentioned that the village and its vicinity had dayschools too - the Stansfelds and Briggs took an active personal part as teachers, providers and innovators. And all this despite the fact that one of the main participants, Henry Briggs's nephew, James Milnes Stansfeld, was said by a gossip to have had a glass eye! At nearby Overton, where he lived, Henry Briggs established a school in 1841, aided by government grant through the British & Foreign School Society. The Tudor-style building stood until the 1960s, but it perhaps closed quite early as a school.

By the 1850s Briggs was chairman at the annual meetings of the Westgate Chapel congregation, and by 1845 and in 1862 he was a subscriber to the funds of the British and Foreign Unitarian Association. In 1854 he chaired the annual meeting of the West Riding Tract and Village Mission Society (a solely Unitarian venture) and his elder son was its treasurer. Father and son offered £20 a year, if nine other persons would each give £10, towards the salary of a second home missionary for that Society, provided that the colliery districts of Castleford, Whitwood and Newton, etc. (sic) were included in his district. The offer was repeated in 1857, but how far it was implemented is uncertain. In 1876 Messrs Pingle and Firth were mentioned as Unitarians of Castleford. Henry Briggs had been a subscriber to this Society as early as 1817. He was also a Unitarian lay preacher, and is shown as being "*planned*" in 1864, in which year he subscribed £5 to the Society and ten shillings to its tract distributing department. He is mentioned as being a one-time missioner at Clayton West. The whole of the Briggs family at this period were active Unitarians - as were the male heads of the family until the death of D.H.C. Briggs in 1974 - and H.C. Briggs, who was living at Dundee at the time, was probably one of the "*various well-to-do English Unitarians ... just settled in Dundee*" whose presence caused the Scottish Unitarian Association to make efforts to revive the Unitarian cause there. He is later said to have been active in the refoundation of the old Stockton congregation when living at Saltburn.

Briggs and Stansfeld were paying £5 a year as pew rent at Westgate Chapel, Wakefield, by 1834, and continued so to do until 1840, when they paid for only the first quarter of the year. Henry Briggs was one of the trustee-opponents of the Reverend John Cameron, the radical and Chartist minister of the chapel who was ultimately got rid of by process of law. In 1844 Briggs, his young nephew J.M. Stansfeld, and Briggs's partner, Charles Morton - who had all been appointed chapel trustees in 1838, although Morton paid no pew rent until 1839 - paid three shillings each for pew rent for the year. In 1845 Cameron was disposed of and Briggs & Stansfeld became major pew tenants again until 1851, after which Briggs and his widowed sister-in-law Mrs Stansfeld paid for different pews. Charles Morton had ceased payment in 1844, but returned in 1851 and continued until he left Wakefield in 1868. Briggs was joined by his sons as pew rent payers in 1856. The elder son paid until 1866, when he was in Dundee, and Archie paid until 1861, when he went to foreign parts. He then returned as a chapel member in 1866 and paid until 1879. Henry Briggs's widow continued the tenancy of her pew until 1882 when the rent was discontinued. The Stansfeld brothers, James and Henry, subscribed "*for the Choir*" in 1857 and 1858, and James had a sitting of his own from 1855, while their mother only gave up her sitting in 1879.

Although Henry Briggs lived into his seventy-sixth year, he suffered ill health during his last years. About 1865, he joined a party of workmen who were haymaking, and, feeling hot from his exertions, he lay on some new mown grass, from which he caught cold and sciatica. The resulting ill health led him first to visit his younger son, Archibald, then residing in sunny Algeria, and subsequently to visit his elder son, H.C. Briggs, then a partner in the mat, matting and carpet manufactory, in Dundee. Harry wrote to his brother on September 25th 1868 that their father was "*seriously ill*", and that old Henry's loss of his false teeth during the journey to Dundee added *"greatly to his discomfort & to his bad looks"*. The old gentleman was afflicted with diabetes during his last few weeks, and he died in October 1868. The funeral took place as directed by his will, with *"no unnecessary expense ... nor any pompous display"*, and he was buried in a freehold plot in the Western Cemetery at Dundee.

Apart from his interests in the various collieries, Briggs had been a director of the Yorkshire Railway Waggon Co. Ltd since its incorporation in June 1863, a major investor in the West Riding Steam Ploughing, Cultivating & Thrashing Co. Ltd of 1862-70, a holder of debenture stock in the Alliance Financial Co. Ltd, and a purchaser of *"certain Cornish Mining Shares ... which turned out to be fictitious"*. A Liberal in politics, he reputedly (see his obituary notice in the *Wakefield Express*) took little part in active political work, and his name does not appear as a member of the Wakefield (Liberal) Reform Association of 1860 in its early years, although he had been active in the anti-Corn Law agitation of the 1840s. He did, of course, serve upon occasion as a township officer on a yearly basis in those townships in which he was a ratepayer. He was an active trustee of Westgate Chapel, Wakefield, and he became related by marriage to Goodwyn Barmby, the Christian Socialist who served as minister at the chapel from 1858 to 1879. He was Superintendent of the Westgate Chapel Sunday School until his death and he was also stated to be a regular visitor of the poor in their cottages. The *Wakefield Express*, the local Liberal newspaper, claimed in its obituary notice that Henry Briggs was *"much respected not only in this locality, but in much of the West Riding and other counties"*.

EXPANSION

The first lease of coal at Whitwood was signed on December 1st 1841, although judging from the situation elsewhere and from the date of commencement of the Whitwood lease, both borings and a trial sinking would probably have already been made to prove the coal to be of workable thickness and quality. The lease was from the Earl of Mexborough, whose country house was at nearby Methley Hall, to Henry Briggs of Overton, described as being an esquire, and to Charles Morton of Normanton, "*Coal Merchant*". It was of the Shale, Main (= Stanley Main) and an upper seam some 20 yards above the Shale, under some 404½ acres of ancient enclosure and some 181 acres of allotments from the common in Whitwood, with ways from the mine to the nearby York and North Midland Railway and to the Aire and Calder Navigation, for 21 years from October 5th 1840. The rent was on an increasing sliding scale, rising to a minimum of £1050 in the 8th to 14th years and then to £1200 for five acres minimum worked in any year. Acreage rents for coal worked beyond the annual 5½ acres were on a sliding scale which again rose to £145 an acre for the Main Coal and £95 for the Shale. No rent was specified for the first year - what coal was worked then was to be taken with that worked subsequently - and power was given to erect and work lime kilns, cottages and coke ovens. Surface land injured, with compensation set at £4 per acre per annum, was to be restored from time to time, or charged at £100 an acre. Briggs and Morton had already built twelve cottages and the cost of them was to be allowed by the Earl from the rent. The lessor, the 3rd Earl of Mexborough, had a home which was upwind of the site of the new colliery, but he was in considerable need of the coal rents as the erstwhile Fenton rents from coal at Methley ceased about this time, the materials of the colliery being advertised for sale in 1843. The third Earl, who "*reigned*" from 1830 until 1860, was for some years one of the MPs for Pontefract. He was also Provincial Grand Master of the Freemasons in the West Riding for several decades, but he left only a modest sum when he died and Methley Park was let in his successor's time.

A renewal Mexborough lease was signed in July 1859 to Henry and Harry Briggs, and allowed both the working of the remaining Stanley Main coal and the carriage of 'foreign' or non-Mexborough coal through the shafts, for 17 years from October 5th 1861, at a minimum rent of £900 a year. The Mexborough Stanley Main coal was to be charged at £145 an acre and the foreign coal was to pay £100 for each five acres until all Mexborough coal was exhausted, when it would become £200 for 10 acres each year. Several areas of coal had already been leased to the partners. Early in the following year, Mexborough leased the Lofthouse or Haigh Moor seam, the Warren House coal and the Stanley Main remaining under some 789½ acres in Methley to Henry and Harry Briggs, J.F. Tonge and William Briggs, with liberty to erect and use coke ovens and lime kilns, and build railways to the Aire & Calder Navigation, the Midland Railway, the York and North Midland Railway and the Great Northern Railway, for 21 years from October 1st

1851 if the Earl lived so long. The rent from the second year was to be a minimum of £880, with £180 an acre for the High Moor and £80 for the Warren House, while the rent for the Stanley Main would be agreed when it was proved to be workable.

In 1857 Henry Briggs and his son agreed to take on a 21 year lease from April 1st of that year from the Earl of Mexborough for the deeper Haigh Moor coals (at around 233 yards, which was almost 100 yards deeper than previous workings) under an area of some 340 acres of their earlier lease of the Stanley Main and Shale coals. The adjoining coals of Sir Thomas Cullum were to be taken, too, and the farm which had been run by the firm since 1840 was to be continued. Presumably the old partners had insufficient capital for the new working, as, in 1858, a new co-partnership deed was drawn up and signed. It was to last for 21 years, the capital was to be £27,548 4s 2d and the interests were to be divided as follows:-

5/8ths	Henry Briggs
2/8ths	H.C. Briggs
1/8th	H.K. Spark.

The colliery's trade was divided into retail, which was coal sold on the North Eastern, Midland and North Western (London North Western or the so-called little North Western) Railways, and wholesale, which was coal sold by water, shipped at Hull, or sold via the Great Northern or the Lancashire and Yorkshire's Wakefield, Pontefract and Goole lines, or carted to Castleford or Wheldon. The retail trade was to be conducted from York or Darlington, and twenty per cent of the profits of that trade were to be regarded as wages, with 1/4th to Spark, the rest to the Briggses.

The partnership of 1858 survived for only a few months, being dissolved in February 1859. The whole concern was then valued at £42,727 and the deed of dissolution contains the unusual provision that Spark should be able to purchase the whole concern, if he so wished, in the period between two and six and a half years after its date. It also mentions the possibility of establishing a connected "*Iron works*", which is interesting in the light of slightly later developments. Connections with Spark continued in various forms, but the colliery connection ceased late in 1859 when the Briggses agreed to acquire Spark's right to purchase the whole business in return for a ten-year contract to sell all their coal from Whitwood and Methley Junction. (This was repudiated by the firm in 1861, and led to a lawsuit.) They also agreed with Spark that, if he would put up part of the capital for the purchase of the Methley Junction Colliery, he might take up a third share in the whole of the colliery business, but this was apparently never implemented. As has been seen, Spark ultimately bought Newton Colliery in 1863 for £9000.

Henry King Spark was in fact a man with wide interests, only a few of which touched upon those of the Briggs family. He was a miner's son and was born at Alston in Cumberland, in 1825. He was a printer (presumably as a journeyman) in Leeds and in Barnard Castle before obtaining a position on the *Darlington and Stockton Times* in 1848. He subsequently became a coal merchant's clerk and then a coal merchant and later still, by *"wise speculation"*, a colliery owner. Achieving a position in local society, he built a mansion at Greenbank in Darlington and became a captain in the Volunteers, although he was ultimately dismissed from that position on account of his neglecting it. He became principal partner in the *Darlington and Stockton Times* and used the newspaper in the Liberal interest. In 1866, 1874 and 1880 he stood unsuccessfully for Parliament against the powerful Quaker interests of the area. In 1875 he sold his mansion and moved to Penrith, becoming a bankrupt in the following year after the failure of the Merrybent and Middleton Tyas Mining and Smelting Co. Ltd, for which the Darlington District Bank was a creditor for £4591. In 1880, when his Parliamentary ambitions were to be unfulfilled for the last time, the *Darlington and Richmond Herald* spoke of him, in the customary manner of rival newspaper interests of the period, as an *"undischarged bankrupt and vainglorious braggart"*, although in fact he was a pioneer of industrial co-partnership and an advocate of old age pensions, and was spoken of as the *"idol of the working classes"*. Perhaps his peccadillo in paying for his own portrait, to be hung in the Town Hall, while claiming that it had been paid for by public subscription, can be forgiven at this length of time. In the late 1860s Spark took over the Yewthwaite Lead (and other minerals) Mine, west of Derwentwater in Cumberland, and *"continued operations for a few years, but not with the same vigour as the former proprietors"*. He also worked the nearby Barrow Mine, although there too he had *"little or no success"*. Spark, a bachelor, lived on until 1899. He was apparently bankrupt again in 1880, when he was at Startforth, a mile from Barnard Castle.

Spark's partnership, short-term though it was, seems to indicate under-capitalisation on the part of the Briggs family when there was a sudden need for cash to open out the lower seam workings at Whitwood, followed by a need for cash to purchase an adjoining coal royalty of Methley Junction Colliery, just to the north.

As capital was still insufficient, money for the new Briggs' purchase was raised by admitting new partners to the whole concern in January 1860, the new capital basis of the concern being arranged as follows:-

	£
Henry and H.C. Briggs, both of Outwood Hall	
value Whitwood Colliery and farm	47,500
new capital	4,500
James Fletcher Tonge of Sowerby Bridge, corn miller	15,000
William Briggs (one of Henry's elder brothers), Halifax, banker	8,000
	£75,000

The capital was to be held in 75 shares at £1000 each, and Archibald Briggs, Henry's younger son, could be admitted to a share in the Henry and H.C. Briggs' interest in the co-partnership. The last two were to receive £1000 a year for their superintendence of the collieries, and the firm was to be known as Henry Briggs, Son and Company. Now, for the first time, the firm became the owner of a colliery village in the accepted sense, as Methley Junction colliery village was a recognisable village, in part built by Burnley, and it stood, virtually complete, until the later 1980s, whereas previous rows of cottages owned by the partners had been scattered indiscriminately (or seemingly so) around the fields close to the pits.

Already some *'foreign'* coal had been leased. From January 1st 1858 the partners took 167 acres of adjoining coal in the Loscoe Grange (Holdsworth) estate, for 21 years plus 10 years' extension rights, and some 25 acres of the same Stanley Main seam from Mrs Heywood, a widow, of Ackton Hall, for 15 years. This latter estate passed by sale to the ubiquitous and frankly unpleasant lawyer, George Bradley, who refused to accept the Briggs' rent cheque when it arrived late in 1873 and declared the lease forfeit in consequence. He later relented, probably as a result of his own continuing chronic shortage of money. Bradley had renewed the lease in November 1869 for 21 years and as for some 80 acres, on terms which were peculiar in Briggs's experience, being a minimum rent of £300 a year, plus payment at £20 per acre/foot thickness of coal up to three feet, and £2 10s 0d per acre/inch above, with £500 down payment on signing the lease. The strange story of George Bradley is told by the present author elsewhere.

Briggs seem to have owned very little surface land in the Whitwood area, having bought only some 2300 square yards on Whitwood Common in August 1853 for £92 6s 6d. At the end of that year, 12 houses were being erected upon this land, adjoining the bank of the mill race. (Details of the Methley Junction estate, which was purchased in 1859 and was both copyhold and leasehold, are given elsewhere in this monograph.) At the end of 1864, as the Whitwood and area coalfield developed further, the partners bought some 10 acres of surface and coal at Normanton Common for £1000 from the vicar of Normanton. By March 1873 three pits had been sunk on this land, to the west of Pontefract Road, a colliery railway had been opened (connecting up with Whitwood Colliery Yard) and two rows of cottages had been built, with probably 19 and 16 houses. Further land and/or coal was purchased or leased in the 1860s and 1870s. In 1869 and 1873 two areas of Normanton vicarage coal were leased at £170 an acre (including some 59 acres of Silkstone or Middleton Main coal at £135 an acre in 1873), while in 1866 and 1870 two areas of Stanley Main coal of about 3½ acres and some 1½ acres in Normanton were bought outright for £450 and £186 respectively. In 1871 another 20 acres were leased at £220 minimum rent and £110 an acre, while in October 1873, 10 acres were bought for £1345 10s 6d, the coal to be got in nine years but without power on the owner's part to make later claim for any subsidence. In December 1871 an unstated area of Stanley Main in Normanton was bought for £460, with underground wayleave included, to be worked in seven years and without, again, subsequent subsidence responsibility on the Company's part. In January 1870 Dame Anne Cullum, whose estate was partly in central Normanton, but also had 57 arces in adjoining Snydale, leased coal in Normanton (the Stanley Main), and the area was extended in 1873. The Cullum leases apparently fell in in 1890, but as early as 1855 the Briggs' partners had leased Cullum houses and land at Whitwood for 21 years, while in 1864 houses and land there were also leased from Amos Cheesbrough and from Benjamin Wilson. In 1871 and 1873 the Company took a lease and made a purchase, respectively, of coal at Woodhouse, in the north western portion of Normanton township and a mile or so beyond Normanton Common, but the Favell estate Stanley Main coal in the western part of Normanton township had been leased in 1865.

Details of some of the acquisitions are given here to illustrate the numbers of owners to be negotiated and agreed with, the geographical spread of the coalfield which was being negotiated for, and the varied terms and types of the acquisitions. Equally, the capital outlay was very large, as, although only relatively few were outright purchases of coal, the minimum rents - and the actual rents - for areas worked were very substantial, although the processes allowed for the long-term future working of the Company. An agreement for a yet further Mexborough lease was signed in December 1874, and now the Silkstone seam under some 600 acres was to be worked, involving another major new development, as the bottom of the Stanley Main best coal lay at some 57 yards in the shafts at Whitwood, while that of the Silkstone was at 420 yards. The new minimum rent was £1440 at £240 an acre, plus the provision of 200 free tons for the landlord in London and £25 an acre for underground wayleave for non-Mexborough coal. Some of the coal might also be sub-let to Pope & Pearson. Eighteen months later, there remained only some 45½ acres of the proved Stanley Main coal to get, and a new lease of it was agreed at £170 an acre, minimum rent £1062 10s 0d, for 14 years from October 1878. The Whitwood Haigh Moor seam was leased in December 1879 and consisted of around 583½ acres in Whitwood township, 13½ acres in Ackton, another 287½ acres in Whitwood, about 15 acres south of the river Calder in Methley, and a dock at Fairies Hill. The coal was leased at £160 an acre, with a minimum rental on seven acres and double agricultural rent for the use of surface land.

Some inter-working of coal between adjoining, but rival, colliery companies, did occur. For example, in 1875 a licence to assign Normanton vicarage coal in Normanton was signed, and in 1887 an agreement to exchange with Rhodes & Terry of Snydale Victoria Colliery, in Snydale township, was reached, the Company taking some 15 acres and giving up about eight. The Snydale situation was in fact a complicated one, as the Company had mineral rights of its own before it took over the extensive collieries (and their mineral fields) hitherto worked as Whitwell Main at Streethouse (Ellison &

Broadbent) and Snydale Victoria (Rhodes & Dalby). The extensive estate of the Torre family of Snydale Hall was partially bored to a depth of some 174½ yards in 1858 to determine the quality, thickness and depth of the coal. In September 1860 the Stanley Main and Shale coals to the east of Windmill Hill Lane were leased for the extended period of 56 years to Rhodes & Dalby, while in 1868 the western part of the Haigh Moor seam was let to Ellison & Broadbent, for 42 years, but, although they entered into an agreement for the coal, no lease was signed.

Upon the sale of Whitwell Main Colliery at Streethouse to the Company in 1873, the latter agreed to take a lease of the Haigh Moor and Silkstone seams, and in 1879, after a proposal to sell Whitwell Main had fallen through, the Company negotiated for those seams under the Stanley Main royalty which were let to Rhodes & Dalby. Whitwell Main proved a failure, and it was described as *"recently closed"* in 1883. Negotiations to buy Snydale Colliery at a similar period failed, but the purchase was made in 1897. At Snydale, leases of other owners' Haigh Moor and Silkstone coals had to be arranged. In 1903 the Company leased a surface plot at Beck Bridge Lane to a Berlin explosives company for 21 years. Of course the Company also took out its own explosives licences, to allow the storage of those necessities, and licences for Snydale survive from 1897.

On part of the Loscoe Grange estate in Ackton township, where coal and clay were leased in January 1858, new shafts were sunk in the early 1870s and a major new colliery developed. This was a working of the Stanley Main seam and sinking had already begun when the Emperor and Empress of Brazil visited the Normanton Iron & Steel Works and the collieries of Henry Briggs, Son & Co Ltd in August 1871 and were taken up the newly-extended colliery railway to the new site. The brickworks, which it also served, were already at work. Although sinking was already underway when the emperor visited, the new colliery was named Dom Pedro after him. This was altered locally to Don Pedro and apparently, earlier, to Pedro Pit. In June 1873 the Stanley Main seam was reached at 120 yards, with no accident occurring during the sinking. The layout of the new colliery was planned by George Robson, the Company's manager, and in October 1880 the story of a ghost in the workings, itself working and walking, seen and heard, appeared in the *Wakefield Express* newspaper. The Company took the lease of the Loscoe Grange mansion into its own hands in 1877.

Much attention was necessarily given to the acquisition of unworked mineral resources. As coal was soon exhausted when it was worked relatively quickly and in large quantities, it was necessary to provide constantly for ample new supplies. Not only had such coals to be got, however, but they also had to be located, negotiated for, proved, leased - little was bought along with the surface - financed, opened out, connected with transport systems, provided with qualified officials and workmen and their houses and social facilities. With the working-out of the upper seams, others, which lay deeper

PLATE III Dom Pedro Pit, abandoned May 1905.

and which were, even if of an equivalent or even better quality, more expensive to open out, had to be worked. As the areas once worked and still working expanded in size, so the number of mineral owners multiplied and there were increased difficulties in regard to underground wayleaves for the *'foreign'* coal carried through one owner's space below ground, frequently to be finally drawn through shafts sunk in yet another owner's estate, and there were of course the continuing difficulties caused by subsidence in areas where thick seams were being worked and where the surface, largely as a result of coal exploitation, was becoming more densely settled with new dwellings and ancillary buildings.

The new Common Pits, lying alongside the Normanton and Castleford road at Whitwood, had been sunk by 1857 and later a long row of good-quality, colliers' cottages, somewhat ambiguously known as the Common Row, was built close to them. The Common Pits had only a short life and the shafts, which were covered until around 1970, have since been filled and fenced. The cottages survived until the early 1970s. A branch railway was built to connect with the Common Pits and later with Good Hope and ultimately with Don Pedro. In the early 1880s, this railway was to have an end-on junction with the new Snydale Branches of the Midland Railway, providing a new connection to the Midland main line, and it was opened in 1885. In the 1860s the firm was stated to rent coal staiths on the North Eastern Railway (of which the York & North Midland, running past the first old Whitwood Colliery, had become a constituent member in 1854) at the majority of that system's extensive number of stations, and to send coal *'abroad'*, shipments being made at Hull and at Goole. The Western European markets were opening in this period as internal industrialisation there was insufficiently provided with native coal, and the Yorkshire coalfield was a major provider of the coal required. More locally, the partners spent £3700 in 1861 in purchasing land alongside the river Aire in Aire Street in Leeds for the purpose of selling coal. John Atkinson, coal merchant, was their agent there in 1864, and part of the freehold was sold in 1868. Negotiations for taking a coal sales office in Bradford was underway in 1873. Occasional references to defaulting coal merchants in the 1860s illustrate something of the spread of customers, with Pontefract, Market Weighton, Snaith, Great Luddington, Cowick and Amsterdam being mentioned.

A further lease was taken from the Rev. G.K. Holdsworth for the coal under his Snydale estate in January 1858, and the firm's lawyers' accounts show that many other smaller coal royalties were being taken from that time forward. The first large undertaking of the new public company was the sinking of a new colliery at Good Hope, Normanton Common, about half a mile to the south of Whitwood. In August 1867 the local newspaper reported that the Company had just finished fitting-up the new colliery and that 62 cottages had been built for the workmen there. In the succeeding year, a further 106 cottages were built. Part of the new labour force was Irish, and resulted in the establishment of Normanton's first Roman Catholic church. During the building of cottages at West Riding Terrace in 1876 (by Mr Webster, as contractor), however, a feud between the English and Irish colliers resulted in a death and a verdict of manslaughter being returned at an inquest held at the Huntsman Inn, which adjoined the new cottages. The firm built an infants' school here, at a cost of £360. An extra locomotive was purchased for working the new connecting railway, which remained in place until the middle of 1969, but Good Hope was worked for only a short period, and was abandoned in 1887. By August 1867 the company owned three locomotives, 550 waggons, 87 chauldren waggons (for internal use), together with 20 stationary engines, two of which were underground.

Coal even further to the south, at Loscoe in the township of Ackton, was sunk to in the early 1870s. The Company's report for the half year ending June 1871 says that the winding engines and temporary pumping apparatus at the Loscoe new winning had been completed, temporary pumps had been erected, and the sinking of the shafts resumed, and it was hoped that the Stanley Main coal, already paid for, would be reached within the next twelve months. As we have seen, in the August of 1871, the Briggs' collieries were visited by Dom Pedro II, Emperor of Brazil from 1831 until his abdication in 1889, and his Empress, who arrived at Normanton Station at 8.15 a.m. and left at 3p.m. Archibald Briggs had become acquainted with the Emperor when travelling in Brazil with his sickly wife and he was also joint owner of some extensive ironworks there. The Emperor and his wife were visiting a number of the most modern industrial installations in England and they were shown over the collieries by Archibald Briggs, who was then managing director. A special train took the party up a new branch line to the Loscoe pits, which the Emperor *"christened"* Dom Pedro Colliery. The Emperor himself was a curious character, described by a recent writer as:-

> *"a philosopher who carried his democracy and his tolerance to logical extremes ... he engaged a republican to tutor his children, and travelled abroad like an ordinary tourist ... He was a scholar of versatility and imaginitiveness, a minor poet of respectable achievement, and a linguistic prodigy ... peering into the secrets of laboratories and indefatigably tramping round factories, museums and the grandiose international exhibitions of the later nineteenth century ...".*

Considerably more work was needed before the colliery could produce coal, and it was not until June 1873 that the pit was at work, working the Stanley Main at 120 yards and anticipating an output of 700 to 800 tons a day. The pit works were laid out by Mr Robson, the Company's manager, and included one of Dubal's patent fans in lieu of the usual furnace-induced air circulation systems below ground. This needed a 40 h.p. steam engine of its own. A lease of clay on the Loscoe estate was granted to the Company in 1869, and a Loscoe Brick & Tile Company was proposed, unsuccessfully, in 1870. A large brickworks was in fact established in 1871 and opened in that year, with one of Hoffman's patent brick kilns, and it may have been these kilns which provided bricks used in the erection of 108 miners' cottages. Dom Pedro opened at the end of the period of great prosperity and the succeeding depression continued into the mid 1880s. The pit closed in 1911, but the Warren House workings there were not abandoned until May 1929 and ventilation continued until the 1960s.

PLATE IV Whitwood Common Row, c.1914-18.

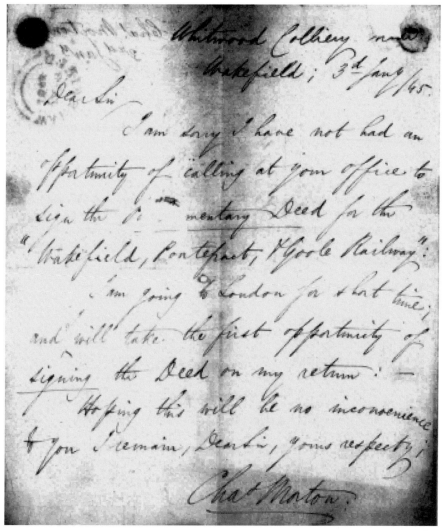

Fig.3 Letter from Charles Morton, Whitwood Colliery, 1845.

Meanwhile, the numbers of employees were growing. In 1867, 975 workmen were entitled to the bonus, and at the time of the Emperor's visit in 1871 there were said to be some 1000 men, producing a maximum of some 2500 tons a day from four pits. These men and their families needed houses.

The colliery business was further extended in 1873, when the company purchased the Whitwell Main Colliery at Streethouse in Snydale township for £55,000. This colliery had been owned by George Ellison, of Birkenshaw, and Henry Broadbent, of Wakefield, who held it under a lease

29

of 1869 from J.W. Torre, owner of the Snydale Hall estate, with a colliery, farm, coal contracts and colliers' cottages. There are now no signs of this colliery, which closed in 1882, with the exception of the Whitwell Main Hotel in Streethouse, though some of the older cottages may date from Briggs' time. A new sinking, to the Silkstone seam, at Whitwood itself was begun in July 1871 and completed in April 1878. These were the works which were deepened to the Beeston seam in 1914 and worked until the abandonment of the colliery c.1970. The sinking of a further large new colliery at Methley, sited between the Navigation and the Midland Railway, began in 1874, again on the Savile estate. The Company's half yearly report of August 1876 reports that the pit was then at work, and the Aire and Calder Navigation had put in one of its basins.

Heavy expenditure had been committed to development work before the onset of the Great Depression during 1874. There seems to be no surviving detail as to what cost what, but at the end of June 1874 recent expenditure at various of the pits then at varying states of development and expansion stood as follows:-

Savile Colliery, Methley

sinking	2720	
sinking pumps	1067	
drainage, road making, levelling for sidings	265	
		4,052

Don Pedro Colliery:

ventilation fan and engines	1033	
ventilation fan engine house	974	
sidings	143	
No.1 reservoir for waterworks	176	
		2,326

Methley Junction Colliery:

Winding engine	492	
.. .. foundations	67	
.. .. boilers	100	
No.1 horse pump extension	75	
special pump	348	
new headgear	374	
new sidings	252	
underground engine steam pipes	57	
new reservoir	67	
		1,832

Streethouse Colliery:

new underground engine	1023	
new boilers	727	
boiler seating and chimney	401	
		2,151
		£10,361

These figures, which obviously represent part of the development expenses in the Company's half year to June 1874, are taken from a few manuscript sheets which were given to the author and which have been torn from a larger volume. Part of the work was done by contract, part by direct labour, and part by a mixture of the two. For example, the Don Pedro fan and its engines were probably by the Grange Iron Co (£900), the Methley Junction winding engine was by Easton & Tattersall (£435) and the special steam pump by Tangye (£275), while the Streethouse underground haulage engines were by Fowlers of Hunslet (£790). At the Savile pit, a part of the sinking was by contract (£414 on account in this half year) and part by sinkers' day work (£436), while Head, Wrightsons provided shaft tubbing at a cost of £323 and the Company cast more at £228, and also apparently provided ring dam castings, walling crib castings and numbers of other castings from its own foundry.

The sinking headgear at the Savile pit, which was obviously of a temporary nature, was largely of Norwegian and Swedish timber, with a little pitch pine and oak, costing in all some £317, while the permanent new headgear at Methley Junction, largely of pitch pine but also utilising some old materials, cost only some £213.

When the partners bought the Methley Junction Colliery in 1860, they not only made their first purchase of such a property and the first of what became a series of such purchases, but they also acquired a colliery which had its own history going back into the 1830s. In September 1833 the Governors of the Wakefield Charities and Grammar School had agreed to let an area of their coal to Messrs Colley & Burnley, and in 1835 a lease of coal was granted by J.P. Heywood of Wakefield to Benjamin Burnley of Newton (near that town) and William Colley of Newton Lane End, both described as colliers. The later lease was of coals down to, and including, a 2 foot 10 inch seam which lay at 90 yards. In 1835 the agent of Colley, Burnley & Co, in which Tottenham Lee (the Wakefield lawyer, worsted spinner and coal owner) was also concerned, wished to negotiate for a wharf in either Thornes Lane or near the Doncaster Road in Wakefield, adjoining the navigable river Calder. In the following year, John Lee's executors' accounts record the receipt of £50 rent from Colley & Burnley for St John's Grove Colliery, while a first rent was due to another coal landlord, David Smirthwaite, on May 1st 1835, at £126 per acre of coal, with a minimum working of three-quarters of an acre a year. It was reported at the time that Lee and Hatfield had laid out £3000 for engines etc connected with sinking the pits on the Pinder Fields for Colley & Burnley.

Colley disappeared early - probably by the time of the trade directory of 1842 - and during 1844-45 legal work was being undertaken in buying out the interests of (probably) Tottenham Lee and John Hatfield. Benjamin Burnley was left as sole proprietor. He had been born at Idle in about 1800 and lived at Horsforth in about 1826 when a son was born. He was in Holbeck

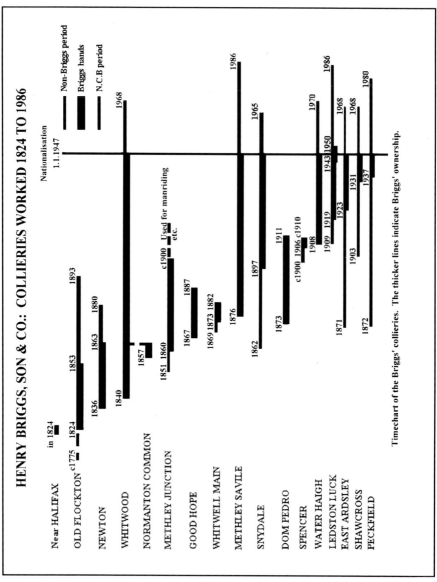

Fig.4 Time-line of the Briggs Collieries.

in about 1829 and at Newton near Wakefield in about 1836. Burnley was also associated with the Beeston Hill Colliery which was operated by Tottenham Lee, Lee's relative Thomas Taylor of Wakefield, and Burnley, who had a quarter share in the estate, the colliery and its colliers' houses. This colliery probably ceased production in 1843, after which the coal was let and the Beeston estate sold in building plots up to at least 1855.

32

Burnley agreed to lease a coal staith on the riverside in Wakefield in 1840, and in 1841 and 1842 he was the purchaser of some of the property of the deceased lawyer and entrepreneur, John Lee. In 1842 he was assaulted at Lake Lock and in 1841 he gave evidence at an inquest following an explosion at his Newton pit, while in 1843 a man fell down one of his pit shafts. In 1844 he took legal proceedings against an Eastmoor collier who neglected *"to attend his work as a Miner and the lawyer was perusing your Agreement with him"*. The magistrates held the agreement to be good, although *"we the lawyers had considerable difficulty as none of the Magistrates appeared to like to interfere"*. The man agreed to return to work. In 1844 further coal was leased, probably in the Lake Lock area, while in 1845 enquiry was made of the York and North Midland Railway as to railway rates for carrying coal to York and Malton. The colliery had apparently envisaged the use of the Aire and Calder Navigation's tramroad to the new canal at Stanley Ferry and, upon its opening at the beginning of 1840, Burnley had *"immediately adopted"* its use, although in what way is not clear. He still had a wharf at Fall Ing in Wakefield in 1847. During 1849 to 1853, Burnley had legal difficulties with subsidence occasioned by his activities, an example being that in September 1853 a *"house at St Johns had shrunk from your having worked the Coal near"*. He owned 20 houses at nearby Newton.

In 1848 negotiations were opened for taking a lease of coal at Methley, on the estate of the Earl of Mexborough of Methley Hall. Burnley was obviously concerned with the situation facing every coal master in that his was an exhausting product, and new resources had to be located, negotiated for and then developed. The coal lease was signed in October 1850, after the appropriate lengthy negotiations for its improvement and development on the landlord's part. Burnley took as partner R.W. Drake, of Durkar House, a man who took an active part in local social life, but who may have been merely a money provider in the colliery. For whatever reason, Drake sold his interest in the partnership's coal and farm leases to Burnley in March 1851 for £716 8s 8d. A year later his household furniture and effects were offered for sale by auction, and by the end of 1852 Drake was dead.

Benjamin Burnley appears to have had difficulty with two of his sons. In 1856 Benjamin junior, then aged about 30, was involved in a case of breach of promise of marriage with a spinster from Cheshire, and damages of £75 were agreed. A house was built at Methley Junction for the father, and as *"lately erected and finished for habitation"*, he let it furnished to his son William, of whom nothing more is heard. Benjamin Burnley's son-in-law, John Thomas Rayner, became Burnley's general manager and ultimately one of his executors. He had been born in London in about 1822 and in 1861 he was living in Methley with his wife and three children, together with a groom, a cook and a housemaid. Burnley died on May 17th 1859 and his will - the last in a whole series which he had made - provided for the sale of the collieries, which in 1851 had employed 138 men and boys. In 1861 they employed 180, made up of 154 men and 26 boys, under Rayner's management, and it was at this time that the collieries were disposed of. The Methley Junction Colliery was sold by Burnley's executors to Henry Briggs & Co, together with the cottages (including Burnley's Row), while Burnley's Foxholes Colliery, where the twin colliers' rows survive, was bought by Rayner and another of Burnley's sons-in-law, William Wood. Rayner died in January 1866 at the age of 44 and the Foxholes business was subsequently run entirely by William Wood into the 1890s. This was apparently the William Wood who was born at Castleford in the 1820s, the illegitimate son of William Moore of Whitwood, farmer, who brought him up and trained him as a land agent.

St John's Grove Colliery was continued under Rayner's management, but after his death it was sold to George Bailey. He sank new shafts, which formed the modern Park Hill Colliery, and St John's closed in 1879. Wood lived into the 1890s, but his colliery, which had old-fashioned machinery, was approaching exhaustion and was abandoned in 1901. His son and partner bought the more modern Glasshoughton Colliery in 1898 for £31,000, but he got into financial difficulties, probably with developments there, and sold it to a joint stock company at the end of 1902 for £115,000.

The Methley Junction Colliery was valued for sale purposes by T.W. Embleton, the great mining consultant, of the Middleton Collieries near Leeds, at £22,267 15s 9d, plus £4013 8s 0d for freehold and copyhold land and five cottages, and in January 1860 it was bought by the Briggs partners for £26,000. A new lease was immediately negotiated with the Earl of Mexborough's agent for 21 years from October 1st 1851, and subsequently in 1863 and 1865 Methley glebe leases were signed for ten and seven years respectively. Further cottages were erected at Methley Junction soon after the purchase, with rows of 12 and 15 having been built by the Briggses by August 1862. Cottages forming three parallel rows survived, with later additions, until the later 1980s. A site for a chapel at Methley Junction was sold to the Primitive Methodists in June 1875.

When the Company purchased the Streethouse or Whitwell Main Colliery, alongside the Lancashire & Yorkshire Railway's Wakefield, Pontefract & Goole line, in 1873, it was a new concern. Working the Stanley Main seam, it had been sunk initially in 1868, and the sinking to 228½ yards, started on February 2nd 1868 and completed on August 19th 1868, was regarded as particularly expeditious. The Scale and Stanley Main seams, respectively some three feet and seven feet thick, were both worked from 1870.

The senior partner in the owning firm of Ellison and Broadbent was George Ellison of Birkenshaw near Bradford, where he was already established as a coal master. Henry Broadbent, who was of Bradshaw in Ovenden near Halifax and a master worsted spinner, was of Wakefield at the time of the sale agreement with Briggs in 1873. The working of the colliery, which had associated colliery cottages, some financed by a female Ellison by the

1870s, was short-lived on Briggs' part and the Scale coal works were abandoned at the end of 1884. The whole venture is shown as *"Old Colliery"* on the O.S. sheet of the early 1890s. The nearby public house, the Whitwell Main, is one of the few such to bear a colliery's name.

The story of this coalfield is inextricably bound up with that of the adjoining Victoria or Snydale Colliery, which was also duly purchased by the Briggses. The coal in the Snydale estate of the Torre family had been bored-to in 1858, although the writer has a shallow boring section of 1818. The 1858 boring reached the Stanley Main at some 174½ yards (sic), but the estate was recognised to be only *"partially bored"* when, in September 1860, J.W. Torre agreed a lease with John Rhodes of Tong and Samuel Dalby of Bradford Moor, coal proprietors, for some 480 acres of the Scale and Stanley Main seams for 56 years from November 1861 at £60 and £120 per acre respectively, and a total minimum rent of £360 a year. The lessees were to have the first chance of leasing other coal in the estate beyond a supposed fault. No subsidence damages were to be paid except in relation to surface buildings. The colliery opened in 1862.

This lease obviously excluded 300 acres or so of the Snydale estate which in March 1869 Rhodes & Dalby were offered on lease, but refused, claiming difficulties with their current workings. In May 1869 they gave up any rights to the further area, which in the same month was agreed to be let to Ellison & Broadbent at £60 and £200 per acre for each seam, and with a minimum rent of £520. It was on this royalty that the Streethouse or Whitwell Main Colliery was sunk, as already described.

The Company agreed to buy Streethouse Colliery in July 1873 for £55,000, and a new lease was agreed with Torre, the term to be for 42 years from April 1st 1874 at £160 an acre a year for the Haigh Moor and £140 an acre a year for the Silkstone seam. The minimum rent for the first five years was to be £500. After that it was to be £1500. Powers were included to abandon any seam of less than 2 feet 6 inches in thickness. The Scale and Stanley Main coals continued to be worked under the 1869 lease. In 1879 the Company applied for a lease of the two top seams under the Rhodes & Dalby area of Snydale Colliery, to allow the formation of a sufficiently large royalty to warrant the cost of major new developments. The latter firm had sunk a shaft to the lower seams, and in 1882 negotiations were in hand for the sale of the Snydale Colliery to the Briggses. However, after the collapse of the negotiations, Rhodes & Dalby worked the deep seams and took powers to make coke and burn bricks in a lease which was to extend to 1917.

ECONOMIC AND SOCIAL EXPERIMENTATION

In the 1850s and 1860s the firm first became involved with a major question which still exercises our capitalist society to a marked degree. Simply stated, the question is that of who is the master. Is it the capitalist or the organised labour force? Henry Briggs was a master born. A radical in religion, but a staid Liberal in politics, he was obviously much exercised in mind - as well as being affected financially - by the rise of colliers' trades unionism. Sometimes his actions were nothing less than cruel as he attempted to prevent the spread of miners' unionism, as, for example, when he ejected 41 colliers and their families from their cottages at Methley Junction in October 1862. A number of other cases of bad feeling also occurred in the early 1860s.

Rules for the Whitwood and Fairies Hill Collieries had been published in 1856 under the provisions of the Coal Mines Act of 1855, and had been printed by George Horridge, the Wakefield Unitarian printer. This was a legal procedure, but it is interesting to note the required payment of two pence per week towards *"the Accident Fund"*, of which the owners were treasurers and for which the workmen were to appoint two of their number to audit the accounts twice yearly. Further rules were printed in 1861 to cover the running of both Whitwood and Methley Junction Collieries. A manuscript set of colliery byelaws of 1857 provide for the surface men working daily from 6 a.m. to 5 p.m. (Saturdays 6 a.m. to 4 p.m.), with one hour for breakfast and lunch. By 1857 prosecutions for leaving work without notice were being dealt with at the Petty Sessions, and in March 1858 the firm's lawyers were advising H.C. Briggs concerning an anticipated strike in consequence of a proposed reduction in the colliers' wages. A few months later, the lawyers advised the firm *"to summon the Ringleaders & you did so"*. The pit concerned, the Common Pit (and this is the first reference to it), had been standing from April 2nd to April 13th 1858, owing to a strike.

Three legal cases between 1862 and 1863 show something of how the workforce was organised. By 1862 the men had their own check-weighman, David Frudd, a chimney sweep turned collier, who lived in Castleford. Documents in the case refer to Henry Briggs and to Harry Briggs, also known as H.C Briggs. In that year the boys who were hurrying (i.e. pushing tubs) were still employed in gangs of four or six, being paid on output (10d a dozen) on Saturdays. The boys divided the money between them at the Robin Hood public house. One boy, who was weak and did not hurry uphill, did not receive as much as the others. The firm's cashier stated that he had paid out nearly £80,000 in weekly wages during the four years he had then held that position. In 1863 an interesting case occurs which refers to a collier, who came from Lancashire and who had agitated for a strike, being given notice, with the nominal two weeks' notice on either side being neglected. He had *"laked"* for twelve months at the Union's expense, but had previously been paid 1s 10d per ton of coal sent to the pit top. The usual earnings were about 4s 6d a day and he provided his own tools.

Relations between masters and men became very bad in the early 1860s, and the following, often-printed letter from a disgruntled collier to Henry Briggs at Outwood Hall, dates from October 1863:

> "Mr. Briggs,
> I will tell you what I think by you. About the struggle you are getting an old man, and besides you are a tyrant, Ould Briggs. Now sirs, what do you think to that. We have stopped 13 weeks already, but I have myself sworn to take your life and your son also. But you shall no live 13 days. Depend on it my nife is sharp, but my bulits is shurer than my nife, and if I can under the time I will by God if it be at noonday when I see you shall have the arra if it be in your charrit like old Abe. Now read that and pray to God to forgive your sins, to be reddy."

It was suggested that the letter was written when its author was drunk, but it illustrates the very bad feelings of the earlier 1860s which led to ejectments, strikes, blacklegs and so forth. It is difficult to apportion blame, but it must be suggested that Henry Briggs, perhaps in particular among the whole of the West Yorkshire coalmasters, was by no means blameless, even though his opposition to Unionism must have been strengthened by his need to give a lead in his position as leader of the Masters' Association. The whole sorry story is told in the first volume of the late Frank Machin's *The Yorkshire Miners* and the events cannot but have been important in leading H.C. Briggs into the profit-sharing scheme of 1864 and the succeeding years.

The deterioration in owner/worker relations was probably a major factor in the introduction of co-partnership and incorporation in 1865 at the initiative of Harry Briggs, but with the approval of his father and/or the other partners. The need to raise further capital was also involved, and it would be fascinating to know if there was any influence, direct or indirect, brought to bear upon the members of the Briggs family by their minister and relation, Goodwyn Barmby, a Christian Socialist and Unitarian minister at Wakefield from 1858 to 1880, who married Harry Briggs's wife's sister.

The events of 1863, a year of massive unrest in the West Riding coalfield, had been traumatic at Whitwood and Methley Junction. In August 1863 the partners applied for 61 ejectment warrants in relation to their workmen, and continued disturbances by the colliers were reported in the following month. A year later, on September 19th 1864, a conference – described as a long one – was held at Outwood Hall, the home of old Henry and Harry Briggs, when the matter of the proposed formation of a limited liability company *"in connection with your collieries"* was discussed with the partners' lawyers, Scholey & Skipworth of Wakefield. By the end of that month, however, John North, who was the junior partner in the law firm of William North & Son of 4 East Parade in Leeds and who had qualified in 1858, had drafted a prospectus which was approved after revision in October 1864. Harry Briggs

COLLIERS WANTED !

TO work in the Methley District, at a Reduction of 7½ per cent. from the old rates; and at

ALLERTON COLLIERY,
(BOWERS AND SONS')

To Riddle for nothing, in beds wet, dirty, and very dangerous—equal to a further Reduction of 15 to 20 per cent., and a great chance of maiming or death. At

KIPPAX COLLIERY,
(LOCK AND WARRINGTON'S)

WEST RIDING & HAIGH MOOR,
(POPE AND PEARSON'S)

FOX HOLES,
(RAYNER AND WOOD'S)

At the Reduction enforced by the Masters' Union; with the further condition that the Colliers are not to unite to Defend themselves. At

WHITWOOD & JUNCTION COLLIERIES,
(H. BRIGGS & SONS)

To be Reduced to Bowers' terms, as soon as their men can be starved out; to be charged a high rent (2s. 6d. and 2s. 8d. per week) for wretched houses, (and with water unfit for horses to drink); to be ejected from house and garden whenever the whim for reduction can be exercised; and generally to lie down, and be peaceably trampled upon, and dictated to, without reply or resistance.

On these FAIR and GENEROUS TERMS,

SUBMISSIVE TOOLS

may be kept at work, for *perhaps* three days a week; and when Coal is very high, they will be required to work excessively, and then be upbraided with earning too much.

DIRTY SLAVES ARE WANTED,

as above, to displace and destroy men who, for simple justice, stand up for fair wages, and the liberty to protect their labour.

For further Information, apply to Mr. RICHD. MITCHELL, Barnsley; and to Mr. JAS. PRICE, Bay Horse Inn, Methley.

August 11, 1863.   BY ORDER.

PRINTED BY F. R. SPARK AND Co.   Leeds.

Fig.5 Spoof recruitment notice, 1863.

was apparently the partner principally involved in the negotiations and the new draft prospectus provided for the incorporation of a company with:

> *"the primary view of securing the co-operation of all those connected with the collieries, either as managers and workpeople, or as customers, and in the earnest hope that a satisfactory solution may be worked out of the difficult problems now occupying so large a place in the minds of political economists and philanthropists, namely the best mode of associating capital and labour, so as to prevent the occurrence of those trade disputes and strikes which so frequently disturb the social relations of our country."*

The collieries were now producing from 5000 to 6000 tons weekly from the Stanley Main (a six foot seam) and the Haigh Moor (some 4 feet 6 inches in thickness). There were two locomotives, over 500 railway waggons and four canal boats, as well as 88 cottages built on the partners' own freehold. It was proposed that the members of the 1860 Briggs' co-partnership would keep two thirds of the capital, and that the business would be fully co-operative, in that half of the profits above 10 per cent would be allotted to the company's employees, and a preference in the allotment would be made first to employees, and then to customers.

In relation to the profit-sharing part of the scheme, the draft prospectus stated that:-

"The principle involved in the adoption of the somewhat novel recommendation thus made would be; Firstly that labour, as represented by the managers & operatives shall receive fair & reasonable remuneration at rates not exceeding the average of those current in the district for similar work - Secondly that capital as

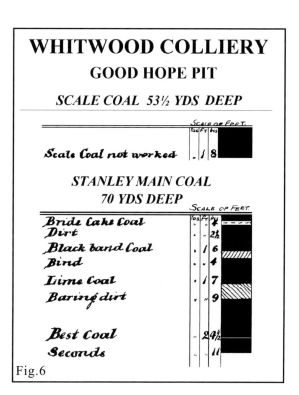

WHITWOOD COLLIERY
GOOD HOPE PIT
SCALE COAL 53½ YDS DEEP

Scale Coal not worked

STANLEY MAIN COAL
70 YDS DEEP

Bride Cake Coal
Dirt
Black band Coal
Bind
Lime Coal
Baring dirt

Best Coal
Seconds

Fig.6

*represented by the shareholders shall receive a fair rate of interest &
profit on the amount embarked in the business, due allowance being
also made for the redemption or restoration of capital invested in
stock or works likely to become worthless, or of diminished value, at
the end of the leases and Thirdly (& chiefly) that the labourer &
capitalist shall equally participate in all extra profits remaining after
the above named appropriation. - The amount thus becoming payable
to the workpeople or managers being appropriated among them as a
percentage on the amount of wages or salaries respectively earned
by them during the year in which the profit shall have accrued. -
The Founders are of opinion that by the adoption (of the) principle
above enunciated the following advantages would be secured. -*

*1st the attainment of a direct & personal incentive to every worker,
whether a shareholder or not, not only to do his own duty but also to
see that his fellow workmen do not neglect theirs.*

2ndly the prevention of causes for strikes among the workpeople.

*3rdly the direct interest of the operatives in the adoption of improved
modes of working, either by machinery or otherwise.*

*4thly the securing of a permanently settled & superior class of
workmen.*

*The attainment of these advantages is especially desirable in coal
mining operations, nearly seventy per cent of the expenditure being
absorbed in wages for work chiefly performed underground under
necessarily imperfect supervision. -*

*Each share will carry one vote. The managing partners of the present
firm will retain the control of the management of the Business as
hitherto on terms to be agreed upon, consulting from time to time
with the directors."*

In fact the original draft prospectus was extensively altered - the essence of
the amended draft is that copied above - and the name of the firm of Scholey
& Skipworth of Wakefield, attorneys, appears on the altered draft. The
draft was then submitted to legal counsel for the settlement of the wording
of the intended Articles of Association. Applications for shares were to be
received by the end of the year 1865, and initially they were taken up as
follows:

Henry Briggs	Outwood Hall	Colliery owner	2960 shares
H.C. Briggs	Outwood Hall		1200
J.F. Tonge	Halifax		1200
James Ingham	Whitwood	Cashier	12
George Robson	Whitwood	Colliery manager	8
Edwin Healey	Whitwood	Agent	8
John Scholey	Wakefield	Solicitor	40
			5428

The original capital was to be £135,000, made up of 9000 shares at £15 each, which were issued at £10 called up. John Scholey paid his deposit, of 10 shillings a share, on 40 shares of £15 each early in January 1865 and paid four subsequent calls to January 17th 1865, when £10 per share had been called. Scholey died on August 15th 1865 and his Briggs' shares were sold at par in the following month to Peter Wroe of Methley, who was to become a director of the firm from 1875 to 1876. Incidentally, Scholey also owned 100 shares in H.C. Briggs's Merrybent Mining Company.

As has been seen, one of the factors behind incorporation was the shortage of capital experienced in relation to the rate of growth of the Briggs' empire, present and intended. The new limited liability company had a nominal capital of £450,000, including the £60,000 capital of the Yorkshire Coal and Steam Ship Company. The difference between the £75,000 of the 1860 co-partnership and the new capital will be noted. In the event, £247,000 was subscribed to the new concern and many

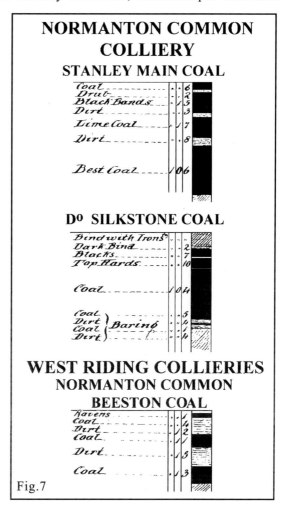

Fig.7

41

outsiders entered the new company. Most of them were simply investors with no experience of the coal industry and some of these investors were on the Board of Directors. A few, like Rowland Childe, M.I.C.E., (1826-86), land and mineral surveyor of Wakefield and son of the colliery engineer at the Flockton Collieries, had a wider knowledge of the coal industry. Indeed, at his death, Childe was described as *"one of the best known mining engineers in the country"*, but he had only a modest investment interest in the new concern, although he also acted for it in a professional capacity.

Henry Briggs himself told the story of the establishment of the co-operative venture in October 1866, when he chaired a great commemorative meeting at Leeds Town Hall, attended by upwards of 1500 shareholders and workmen, *"with their wives and sweethearts"*. Also there were Thomas Hughes and Prof. Fawcett, two strongly supportive Members of Parliament, both of whom spoke, and other supporters of the cause, who were described as *"other distinguished friends of co-operation"*. A long report of the meeting appeared in the *Wakefield Guardian*, a short-lived radical newspaper, and was reprinted as a pamphlet. A special train took the crowd to Leeds, where a procession, containing two bands, was formed. The Oddfellows of the area wore their blue scarves and carried two banners. At the Town Hall, the meeting was preceded by a tea, while the great Dr Spark performed upon the Town Hall organ inside, and a band played outside.

> *"The Chairman, who on rising was loudly cheered, said - My friends, as chairman of the Whitwood and Methley Co-operative Collieries, I have much pleasure in taking the chair at this great meeting. I trust all present have a strong sense of the importance of the object which has called us together, namely, the solution of the great problem whether any plans can be devised and adopted to unite the two great interests which are so frequently considered to clash, and to be antagonistic to each other, namely, capital and labour. (Hear, hear). Our firm has attempted that solution - (Cheers) - and we are met to celebrate and commemorate the first year's successful working of our collieries under the co-operative system and principle (renewed cheers). The motto and device on your banner to-day shortly intimates the principle on which we have founded our undertaking - "Capital and Labour hand in hand." (Loud applause). I must briefly state that this public meeting takes place at the earnest desire and wish of our employees. It is to gratify them that we have waived our own preference for a more modest gathering. It might be thought that in calling the present meeting we were actuated by vain glory and love of display, but I am certain all such ideas will be dissipated when I state that this demonstration takes place alone at the earnest wish of our men (applause). We acceded to their wish also because we thought that public attention ought to be called to the co-operative principle, where it has been so far successfully carried out, in the hope that others, finding that our plans have more than answered expectations,*

may be induced to make similar efforts (cheers). We rejoice, this being a public meeting, that we are favoured with the presence and aid of gentlemen who are conspicuous friends of the working classes, and particularly by the presence of two members of Parliament - (cheers) - who have put themselves to much trouble to attend and take part in the proceedings. We have had letters of apology from others whom we expected, but as the hour is so late I will not read them, but will only, in conclusion, express the great satisfaction it gives me and my partners, my sons who are present, to see our work people at this great social gathering, particularly under the present circumstances. We heartily bid you welcome, and cordially hold out to one and all, the hand of fellowship. (Great cheering). The Chairman then introduced Mr H.C. Briggs, managing director of the Company, who said, - My friends - for so, judging from the many familiar faces around me, I think I may address you (cheers), - as one of the directors and originators of the Company whose anniversary we are met to celebrate, I can most cordially second the words of welcome which have fallen from our chairman. I am delighted that at last we have aroused sufficient interest among our workpeople to induce them to come all together on such an occasion as this. As there are many who are unconnected with the collieries here tonight - some who have come from a feeling of sympathy with the principle of co-operation and some perhaps who have come from a feeling of curiosity to know what all this great stir is about, I will briefly state our present position, and the principles upon which we have been working. All who are familiar with the commercial undertakings in this district will, I think, be fully acquainted with the name of our firm in connection with the coal trade of the West Riding. (Hear, hear). I believe I may say that our chairman is one of the oldest representatives of that trade in the West Riding, and I think that you will all say perhaps we have come in for more than our fair share of abuse in connection with the unhappy disputes that have taken place between employers and the employed. Certainly for some years we seemed to live in a state of perpetual warfare. That was a source of great anxiety to ourselves, and likewise a source of very considerable pecuniary loss. In fact things came to such a pass that we were determined, if possible, to devise some plan whereby the apparently conflicting interests of employers and employed might be reconciled. (Hear, and cheers). I say apparently, because I am convinced in my own mind that those interests, in the broadest point of view, are identical (applause). I feel quite certain that there can be no permanent prosperity to the workmen unless there is equal prosperity to the employers (cheers). It may be possible for trades' unions and for strikes to temporarily build up a rate of wages, but they cannot maintain that rate unless the employer is obtaining a fair remuneration for the capital he employs (hear, hear). I cannot but think, therefore, that the question of reconciling the interests of capital and labour is

Fig.8   **SIMPLIFIED SECTION OF STRATA AT**
WHITWOOD COLLIERY

Date of sinking, to Silkstone 1873, to Beeston 1912
Height above O.D., 68.72 feet. Dip of strata, 1 in 50 south

	Yd	Ft	Ins	Yd	Ft	Ins
Soil, clay & bind	18	1	4			
COAL	0	0	7			
				18	1	11
Spavin, shale & bind	8	0	7			
CAT COAL	0	1	6			
				27	1	0
Spavin, shale & bind	20	1	11½			
SCALE COAL	0	1	6			
				47	2	7½
Spavin, stone & bind	20	1	11½			

STANLEY MAIN SEAM —

	Ft	In			
Bride cake coal	0	2			
Clod	1	4			
Coal (Black bands)	1	4			
Dirt	0	2			
Coal (jumpers)	1	3½			
Baring dirt	0	2½			
Best coal	1	0	1	2	6

	Yd	Ft	Ins	Yd	Ft	Ins
				57	0	9½
Spavin, stone & galliard balls	5	1	0½			
COAL	0	2	0			
				63	0	10
Spavin, stone & bind	8	0	3			
COAL	0	0	10			
				71	1	11
Spavin, ironstone & bind	66	2	2			

WARREN HOUSE COAL —

	Ft	In			
Coal	1	3½			
Dirt	0	2½			
Coal	1	1½			
Dirt	0	1½			
Coal	1	8	1	1	5

	Yd	Ft	Ins	Yd	Ft	Ins
				139	2	6
Spavin, sandstone & galliard balls	91	2	7			

HAIGH MOOR SEAM —

	Ft	In			
Coal(Tops, best)	2	8			
Dirt	0	8½			
Coal (Bottoms)	0	10	1	1	2½

	Yd	Ft	Ins	Yd	Ft	Ins
				233	1	4
Spavin & bind	8	0	10			

HAIGH MOOR SEAM —

	Ft	In			
Coal(fine bright)	0	10			
Black dirt	0	6	0	1	4

	Yd	Ft	Ins	Yd	Ft	Ins
				242	0	6
Spavin, ironstone & thin coal	16	2	9½			

	Yd	Ft	Ins	Yd	Ft	Ins
LIDGETT COAL—						
Dirt and Coal	0	2	7			
				259	2	11
Spavin, bind, ironstone & thin coal	69	2	10			
FLOCKTON THICK COAL	0	1	4			
				329	2	9
Spavin, bind & sandstone	13	0	2½			

DOGGY COAL—

	Ft	In
Coal	0	8
Dark spavin	3	3
Coal	0	2
Dark spavin	0	9
Coal	0	1½

	Yd	Ft	Ins	Yd	Ft	Ins
	1	1	11½			
				344	1	11
Spavin, bind, conglomerate & stone	42	2	5			
MIDDLETON LITTLE COAL	0	2	0½			
				388	0	4½
Stone, bind, ironstone & shale	30	1	10			

SILKSTONE (MIDDLETON MAIN) COAL —

	Ft	In
Coal hards	1	2
Dirt	0	2
Coal (gas)	3	0
Whetstones	0	8
Dirt	0	1
Cat coal	0	1½

	Yd	Ft	Ins	Yd	Ft	Ins
	1	2	2½			
				420	1	5
Spavin & brown stone	0	1	8			
WHEATLEY LIME COAL —						
Coal and dirt	1	0	2			
				422	0	3
Bind, spavin & shale	8	0	4			
MIDDLETON ELEVEN YARDS COAL—	0	1	6			
				430	2	1
Bind, spavin, rock & shale	14	1	10			

BLOCKING COAL—

	Ft	In
Coal	0	7½
Clunch	4	10½
Coal	1	5

	Yd	Ft	Ins	Yd	Ft	Ins
	2	0	11			
				447	1	10
Clunch, bind, ironstone balls & shale	52	0	6½			

TOP BEESTON COAL —

	Ft	In
Coal	2	9
Dirt	0	5
Coal	0	8½

	Yd	Ft	Ins	Yd	Ft	Ins
	1	0	10½			
				501	0	3
Spavin	1	0	10			
				502	1	1

Based on the section in M.A. Wilkinson's (Ed.) *Sections of Strata of the Yorkshire Coalfield* (Sheffield: Midland Institute of Mining Engineers, 1950)

45

one of the greatest questions of the day. (Hear, hear). To my mind it is a much more important question even than the great question of Reform - (applause) - which at the present moment is agitating the working men of England. Look at the ruin and desolation that is impending in a hitherto extraordinarily prosperous district - the iron making district of Middlesboro'. That has entirely arisen from the conflict between employers and employed, and I am quite sure that we who have suffered so much from those evils are perhaps the best qualified to suggest some plan for mitigating them, and hope may, I feel certain, that the plan we have adopted is the one that will attain the very desirable end. (Cheers). We began on July 1st 1865, to work under this new principle, and by that principle we in the first place paid, or stated that we would pay, a rate of wages equal to the average rate of the district. We would not pay more and we would not pay less. That was the first payment that was made out of the produce of the collieries. In the second place we determined to pay a certain dividend to the capitalist - to the shareholders - and that dividend was fixed at 10 per cent. We considered that the capitalist was as much entitled to receive his 10 per cent as the worker was to receive his wages for his work. But then we come to the novel part of the arrangements, which was, that if the profits exceeded 10 per cent on the capital, then that we should divide that excess between the labour and the capitalist. (Applause). The division of any portion which might thus pertain to the labourer was given as a percentage on each man's earnings during the year. On that principle we have been working for the last 15 months. We certainly during that time met with a good deal of abuse. Our motives have been impugned and our good faith has been questioned. But it is said that "nothing succeeds like success" and I think I may say that the bonus of £10 or £5 which many of you have received has been a proof of our success, and I think I may also say that the twelve per cent we have paid to our shareholders has equally been to you an earnest of success (applause). I may further state, as a proof of success, that the dividend which I, as a partner in that colliery, have received during the last year, notwithstanding that we have paid £1,800 to the working men, has been a larger return than I have received from the colliery previously even in the most prosperous years. (Cheers). We don't pretend that we propounded our scheme solely from philanthropic motives. We believed that it would pay. There is tangible proof that it has paid, and I believe that it will continue to pay, and that you will, during the current year, receive a yet more handsome amount of bonus than you did during the last. (Cheers). I am quite certain it is in your power to accomplish this, because we have not had that amount of support hitherto that we had reason to expect. But from what we have seen we have good reason to anticipate better things in the future. I regard such companies as ours as a great commercial training school for the working men of this country. (Hear, hear). I am quite certain that none of you in this hall who co-operate with one another in promoting the prosperity of such a company as ours can do so without benefiting yourselves both intellectually, and in a pecuniary point of view. I believe the plan we have inaugurated is destined to spread far and wide, and to become the means where by the working men of England may gain that position in society which for my own part I sincerely hope they will obtain. (Loud cheering)."

Later in the evening, H.C. Briggs was presented with a testimonial and a silver epergne, paid for by the employees of the collieries. Darnton Lupton of Leeds, the cloth merchant, ex-mayor, philanthropist and member of Mill Hill Chapel, who was then aged about sixty, was the last major speaker. What he had to say was short, but significant:

"If he were called upon to state what had been during the forty-five years the most unsatisfactory business, he should say the coal trade in the West Riding of Yorkshire. It had been, year after year, adversity for the masters; it had been turn-outs, lock-outs, strikes, and wrath, malice, and bitterness between the masters and the employed. They were, therefore, under the greatest possible obligations to any gentleman who could propound a scheme which put an end to such a state of things as that."

There had been difficulties earlier in persuading the men of the overall value of the scheme, and the prospectus issued in November 1865 had brought initially only a small response. A few of the men, including some who had been hitherto implacable opponents in trade disputes, paid up for shares or formed share-clubs, with a weekly 1s 3d payment, but others, described as *"a large portion* [who] *put no faith in the good intentions of the founders of the company"*, had to be persuaded. It was suggested at the time by the management, doubtless with some element of truth, that the initial euphoria on the part of the men with regard to the scheme had been dispersed, as:-

"doubts began to arise in their minds, promoted in the first instance by the paid agents and lecturers of the Miners' Trades Unions, who began to fear that if the co-operative company succeeded, strikes would cease, and their employment come to an end."

In May 1865, therefore, Harry Briggs issued a detailed, reasoned prospectus to the workmen, which seems to have had some success and which was followed, coincidentally, by a period of good trade which allowed an even more appealing 12% dividend for shareholders and £1800 to be paid into the men's bonus fund at the end of the first year's working from July 1865. Business continued good and the men's interest in the financial advantages of the scheme increased. Many of them also availed themselves of the loans offered by the company to enable them to build cottages for themselves on plots of freehold land, offered for sale by the company *"at a low rate"*.

The circular letter to workmen penned by Harry Briggs is long and detailed, setting out the specific financial advantages which the scheme offered to them, but also pointing out how they could contribute personally to the monetary well-being of the company:

> ... *I think it must be clear to all of you that these results are well worth striving for, and therefore proceed secondly to point out how it is within the power of each and every one of you to assist in realising them.*
>
> *1st. It is within the power of you who are colliers, by each endeavouring to get the coal as large as possible, to diminish the proportion of slack 3 or 4 per cent, or, on an average production of 5,000 tons per week, to get 150 to 200 tons of rough coal which otherwise would be cut into slack. As we can sell large coal at three shillings per ton higher price than slack, the saving in this particular alone, would amount to about £30 per week, or £1,500 per year.*
>
> *2nd It is of equal importance that the various qualities of coal should be carefully separated below ground. You must all be aware that when inferior coal is mixed with best coal in one corf it is necessary to sell the whole of the coal contained in that corf, at an inferior price. Hence arises a sacrifice of at least 2s. per ton in the selling price. If each of the coal getters employed at the collieries were, by extra care in sorting the coal, to prevent this sacrifice of price on only two corves per week, that alone would amount to 2s per ton on 300 tons, or £30 per week, equalling £1500 per year. The banksman may also do much towards effecting a saving under this head by paying proper attention to the tipping and Loading of the coal on the surface.*
>
> *3rd It is quite within the power of almost every man employed about the collieries, to prevent the waste of various stores and materials, especially wood, oil and rail. I have heard it remarked that every stall-man might, by proper care, save at least one puncheon or prop per week, This is certainly much within the limit, but that alone would amount to about £6 per week, or upwards of £300 per year. When it is considered that the value of the prop wood used at the collieries reaches upwards of £1,800 a year, it is evident how much scope there is for saving on that item of expense.*
>
> *4th Much may be done towards promoting the general prosperity of the undertaking, by every man and boy endeavouring not only to do his own duty but by seeing that in times of depression in trade. Remember also that many of the expenses of [a] colliery are the same whether a large business, or a small one, be done. I might go on to point out many others' methods whereby you can contribute to the prosperity of the undertaking in which we are mutually interested. I trust, however, that what I have already said is sufficient to induce*

you not only to think on the subject, but to act upon the suggestions I have thrown out, and I would only remind you, in conclusion, that the eyes of many of the most earnest well-wishers of the working classes in England are fixed upon you and your mode of receiving our proposal. The plan upon which we have founded our company is an entirely new one. Throw aside suspicion and distrust, and give it a fair trial, and I am confident that we shall none of us regret its adoption.

I can only repeat what I have frequently said to many of you that our sole object in making the proposal is to realize a plan whereby a better feeling between employers and employed may be promoted, and the interests of the two classes as far as possible identified. If that object be attained, not only we, but future generations, will have reason to bless the day when our project was propounded.

I am
Your true friend
H. CURRER BRIGGS.

Whitwood Colliery,
Near Normanton.

A minor set-back occurred when the Registrar of Companies refused initially to register the new concern *"as there was already a registered firm under the same name"*, making one wonder what name had been proposed, but registration eventually went through under the title of Henry Briggs, Son & Co. Ltd in April 1865, and the first meeting of the shareholders was held in the September of that year. By the memorandum of association, a board was nominated which in fact largely met with the approval of the shareholders, and retained much of its membership for a decade:

			director to
1865	Henry Briggs	Outwood Hall	1868 (death)
1865	H.C. Briggs	Outwood Hall	1881 (death)
1865	J.P. Tonge	Sowerby Bridge	1865
1865	John Olive	Woolford near Bury	1867
1865	Robert Hollings	Methley	1873
1865	George Robson	Whitwood	1880
1865	James Ingham	Whitwood	1868
-	Richard Tonge	Manchester	1872-1906
-	S.H. Tonge	Sowerby Bridge	1872-1886
-	Archibald Briggs		1869-1880
-	Thomas Murgatroyd		1869-1873

Scholey & Skipworth of Wakefield were the firm's lawyers and Leatham, Tew & Co. its bankers. As before, Henry and Harry Briggs managed the business. Harry was the first managing director, holding that office from 1865 to 1868 and from 1876 to 1881. He was also chairman from 1868 to his death in 1881.

The capital structure of the new company was 9000 shares of £15 each, giving a total of £135,000. Of these, 5360 were taken by the old partners. There was a call of £10 on each share, a capital of £90,000 thus being raised. Early in 1866 Harry Briggs proposed raising money for building purposes by debentures, powers to raise £10,000 being given by the articles etc of the company. The money was needed to build houses for the new pit on Normanton Common and for other works rendered necessary *"by the increasing trade of the Company"*. The debentures were to be for three, five or seven years and at five per cent. These monies soon proved quite insufficient and in 1867, in view of further required expenditure upon cottage building and as shares for the workpeople were now allotted, 1000 new £15 shares were issued at a premium of £2 10s 0d and £10 called up. One hundred of these at least were reserved for employees who did not already own five shares or more, with preference being given to men who were not already shareholders. The remainder were to be issued on a pro rata basis to shareholders. By 1871 the paid up capital was £104,716 10s 0d. The ensuing decade of both enormous expansion and economic depression in the coal - and other - industries witnessed an increase of some 150% to £266,934, plus debentures for £59,800, and by 1913 the issued capital at £327,875 was a further increase of some 25 per cent.

The first report of the directors was issued early in January 1866, and printed. It commented that, after a hot summer (which had been poor for domestic coal sales), trade had picked up and in the last two months of 1865 production was some 12% above that of a similar period in the previous year, enabling prices and wages both to increase. An interim dividend at 10% per annum was recommended. As a greater output of coal was required, the sinking of a new shaft to the Stanley Main coal had just been completed, and 400 shares, hitherto reserved, were to be issued at £11 a share (i.e. with a £1 premium), with a preference given to applications from existing shareholders, customers and employees, the £1 premium being used to form the nucleus of a reserve fund. A most interesting comment relates to the workmen's attitudes to the co-operative system's introduction:

"Your Directors are glad to be able to report, that, although in the commencement, much opposition was experienced to the co-operative system under which the Company is working, they find that opposition is gradually diminishing, and they believe that their workpeople are, by degrees, gaining a juster appreciation of the advantages offered to them. This remark is particularly applicable to the miners employed in the Stanley Main Seam, who have refrained from that restriction in their production of coal, which has been so general among those working at other Collieries in the neighbouring district."

The directors' report for the second half of 1867 shews a 15% increase in coal sales and the issue of 760 new shares at a premium of 25%. A dividend of 10% per annum was proposed.

HENRY BRIGGS, SON & Co.,

LIMITED.

WHITWOOD, HAIGH MOOR, & METHLEY JUNCTION COLLIERIES.

REPORT OF THE DIRECTORS—ISSUED 6th JANUARY, 1865.

Your Directors have great pleasure in reporting, that during the half-year ending on the 31st December last, the progress of the Company has been generally satisfactory.

The unprecedented heat of the weather during the earlier months of that period, unfortunately interfered seriously with the demand for Coal for household consumption; recently however, the prosperity of Trade generally has given a great impetus to the demand for Coal, so much so, that your Directors have found it impossible to supply all the wants of their customers, notwithstanding that the production of the Collieries has, during the months of November and December last, been increased about 12½ per cent, compared with that of the corresponding months of the previous year.

Your Directors have therefore been enabled to make some increase in the selling prices of Coal, and to give an advance in wages to the men employed by the Company.

It is not proposed to make a complete valuation of the Stock at the Collieries, so as to ascertain *precisely* the profits realized, until the termination of the financial year, on the 30th of June next; but after carefully estimating the result of the business already transacted, your Directors feel themselves justified in recommending the declaration of an Interim Dividend, at the rate of 10 per cent. per annum, for the past half-year, payable on the 14th of February next.

Your Directors have good reason to believe that the increased demand for the produce of the Company's Collieries, is of such a permanent character as to render it most advisable to take immediate steps to largely increase their productive powers before next winter.

In order to assist in the attainment of this end, they have just completed the Sinking of a New Shaft to the Stanley Main Seam; and have also resolved to increase the Working Capital, by the issue of the 400

Fig.9 The directors of the new limited liability company issue their first report to the shareholders.

"The Co-operative system upon which the Collieries are conducted, continues to give the Directors every satisfaction, and they are anxious to increase the number of shareholders among the workmen."

The report for the first half year in 1871 (the company's sixth year) refers to increasing sales, only held back by the large output of coal throughout the district; the opening of the Loscoe Brick Works, with a Hoffman's patent kiln (costing £4731 13s 0d) and a large demand for bricks; the completion of winding engines at Loscoe and the resumption of shaft sinking there. The value of the colliery stock was now £111,763 16s 1d, plus the value of a farm which was £6663 6s 10d. Following the company's policy of lending money to their workmen for building cottages on freehold land, £1544 19s 3d was advanced for that purpose in the half year to June 1871.

The financial success of the business was immediate. Ten per cent was being divided from the beginning of the new company, and this rose to a very handsome 25% in the early 1870s. The onset of the economic depression in 1874 caused dividends to drop dramatically, however, and in the mid 1880s there were no dividends at all:

	Per cent		Per cent
1873	25	1879	2½
1874	20	1880	2½
1875	11	1881	2½
1876	10	1882	nil
1877	6	1883	-
1878	3	1884	nil
		1885	nil

For a number of years the Company paid bonuses on wages to its workmen, both shareholders and non-shareholders, differentiating between top and bottom men. In the first year of working, from July 1st 1865, £1800, being 2% on capital, was used to form a workman's bonus fund, which at the end of the year was used to pay 10% on the year's earnings to working shareholders and 5% to others. The succeeding figures of percentages paid on wages were:

	Shareholder		Non-shareholder	
	surface	underground	surface	underground
	%	%	%	%
1866 all pits alike	10	10	5	5
1867 ..	12	8¼	8	4¼
1868 ..	10¾	5¼	9	3½
1869 ..	7½	7½	5	5
1870 ..	4½	4½	3	3
1871 ..	4½	4½	3	3
1872 ..	9	9	6	6
1873 ..	22½	15	17½	10
1874 Stanley Main pit	6	4½	4½	3
Junction pit	6	4¼	4½	2¾
Haigh Moor pit	6	4	4½	2½
Streethouse pit	6	3½	4½	2

Bonus champions, non-shareholders, were identified and paid as follows:

		£	s	d
1866	David Newton ... on earnings of ...	109	8	9½
1867	Joseph Hough	119	17	6½
1868	James Dunford	108	5	10
1869	Thomas Fawcett	106	11	6
1870	James Dunford (again) and Job Hartley	116	10	11
1871	Samuel Cawthra	114	8	0
1872	John Stinson	134	3	11
1873	Isaac Ramskill	186	11	2

Meanwhile, topmen's wages, as well as those of the colliers and other underground men, changed with the changing fortunes of the industry:

9/11/1871	a regular adjustment	
6/06/1872	advance of	15%
20/03/1873	..	10%
4/03/1875	reduction of	7½%
3/08/1876	..	7%

The perhaps complex factors which together led to the abandonment of the profit-sharing scheme are well stated by D.F. Schloss in his Report to the Board of Trade's Labour Department of 1894:

"In 1872 the price of coal and the rate of colliers' wages rose rapidly - the advances in wages granted to the miners (including those employed by the company) being an increase in the aggregate of from 27½ to 30 per cent upon their standard rate; and it was thought proper to increase the minimum rate of interest on capital from 10 to 15 per cent, the first division of profits on the new basis taking place in relation to the year ending on June 30th 1873; and this basis was maintained during the rest of the period during which the profit-sharing scheme was in force. The total amount received by the employees as bonus was as follows:

		£
Year ending June 30th 1866	*-.-*	*1,800*
1867	*-.-*	*2,700*
1868	*-.-*	*3,150*
1869	*-.-*	*3,462*
1870	*-.-*	*1,740*
1871	*-.-*	*1,745*
1872	*-.-*	*5,250*
1873	*-.-*	*14,256*
1874	*-.-*	*6,048*
Total	*-.-*	*40,151*

Fig.10 Share certificate for Henry Briggs, Son & Company Limited.

Thus, during the nine years in question the average amount received as bonus was about £4,460 a year. What the average ratio of bonus to wages during this period was is not stated by the authorities consulted, though these give the ratio for 1865-66 as 10 per cent in the case of shareholding, and five per cent in that of non-shareholding employees, and the ratio for 1866-67 as 12 per cent in the case of shareholding employees and eight per cent in the case of non-shareholding, while it would seem that the bonus divisible for 1871-72 was at the rates of nine and six per cent. It is stated that in 1868 the number of persons employed in these collieries was 989 adults and 214 boys, and that in the early part of 1869, out of 989 adult workmen, 144 held between them 178 shares, equal at par value to £1780. From the first adoption of the profit-sharing scheme there had been a committee of the workmen, called together from time to time to give advice in respect to improving the processes of coal mining and, although the workmen had no control over the financial operations of the company, yet as the accounts were verified each year by a public accountant, chosen by the shareholders, the employees had always a full knowledge of the affairs of the business. In 1869 one of the workmen share-holders elected by his fellows, was given a seat as one of the board of five directors. It will be seen that the arrangements made to carry out the method of industrial partnership were in many respects singularly complete; and their

54

effect upon the conduct of the workmen was for some time considered to be very satisfactory. A spirit of harmony between employers and employed was developed, such small disputes as arose being amicably settled without loss of time; the coal was got in a more careful manner; there was a considerable saving in timber used for props, etc. The men showed a willingness to work extra hours when this was asked of them in the interests of the business, and generally were readier to obey orders than before the introduction of profit-sharing. The circumstances which led to the abandonment of the method were briefly of the following nature. Messrs Briggs had hoped that profit-sharing would be accepted by their workmen as a substitute for trade union organisation, they, on their part, abstaining from joining any combination of employers for the regulation of wages. Until the summer of 1868, the workmen seemed to enter into these views, but at that time a growing desire to join the union began to manifest itself, on the ground that, as the company agreed to pay the average weekly wages of the district as well as a share in the profits, and as the union tended to raise these wages, it was to the interest of the workmen to aid in that endeavour. In 1872, after the directors had fixed upon August 19th for the annual meeting of the shareholders, they received a notice stating that a great meeting and demonstration of the Miners' Union was to take place on that day, and requesting that work at the pits should be stopped in order to enable the men to attend. Thereupon the managing director, Mr Archibald Briggs, issued notices to the effect that those who stayed away from work on 19th August would forfeit all claim to bonus for the future, and must take their chance of losing the bonus for the past year, since it lay in the power of the shareholders to settle what bonus was to be given and to whom; and the men were told in plain terms that they had to choose between profit-sharing and trade unionism. About one-third of the men stayed away from work, and were deprived of bonus until reinstated the following Christmas. During 1873, a year in which the coal trade was very prosperous, the relations between Messrs. Briggs and their men, though not so good as before, were fairly satisfactory; but in 1874 a dispute arose about the use of "riddles" for sifting the coal in the pits. The use of riddles underground had, for reasons into which it is unnecessary to enter here, long been a grievance in the eyes of the Yorkshire miners; during the fat years, when coal was so much sought after that even smudge was saleable, the men had been allowed to send up the coal unsifted, a slight reduction being made in their tonnage rate of wages. Now that prices were falling, the employers wished to revert to the use of the riddle in their pits; but the trade union declared that never again should riddles be introduced; and Messrs. Briggs' men for some time declined to use them. The events above described did not, however, lead at once to the abolition of the industrial partnership system. At the meeting of shareholders held in August 1874 it was decided not entirely to abandon it, but to give it one more chance, modifying, however, the rules regulating the distribution of the bonus, and making these rules more stringent. Not long after this Messrs. Briggs, in common with the other employers of the district announced their intention of reducing the men's wages. This reduction the miners, including those employed by Messrs. Briggs, declined to accept, and a strike of four weeks' duration ensued. As the direct consequence of this fact, the final step was taken, and a resolution passed at the half-yearly meeting of shareholders held in February 1875, that the payment of a bonus on the industrial partnership principle should be discontinued. Many of the men themselves had expressed a wish to the same effect, having an idea that we were in some way merely keeping back a portion of their wages to be probably (but not certainly) returned to them, at the end of the year; and they said they would prefer to be paid precisely the same wages, and be put on the same footing as men at other collieries.

"In connection with this case it is worth noting that the system adopted did not partake of the nature of a definite binding agreement between employers and employed, since the shareholders might (as will have been seen) at any time, at their mere caprice, refuse to vote the bonus, and might thus deprive the men of the share in the profits earned during the past year; that the initial rate of dividend reserved to the shareholders before any division of profits in favour of the employees could take place was raised by 50 per cent when wages advanced, but no proposal appears to have been made to reduce it when a reduction in wages was proposed; that in 1873 a sum of £30,000 was taken out of the last year's profits and invested in a new mine, the shareholders getting new shares in respect of the purchase, but the employees losing £15,000 of bonus, which would otherwise have come to them as their share of this £30,000; and that the employees' share in profits was further diminished, because (as it is stated) large sums were placed to depreciation and reserve funds, altogether out of proportion to what is usual. On the whole, the fact that the abandonment of profit-sharing in this case gave rise to no great regret on the part of the collier's concerned is not very difficult to understand."

Naturally, those workmen who had bought shares under the scheme retained them, some indeed being so owned until the winding-up of the Company in 1952, long after Nationalisation.

The onset of the depression in the coal trade - itself, obviously, mirroring a national depression in industry - is well and simply illustrated in the instance of the Briggs's concerns by a list of dividends paid. The increasing depression is also indicated by the worsening relations between masters and men and by the rise of trade union membership among the latter. The profit-sharing scheme of the firm was abandoned in 1875 and the worker-director scheme in 1886. By 1885, the Briggs family owned only one quarter of the capital in the concern, although members of the family were to continue to hold the most senior positions within it until Nationalisation in 1947.

By 1889, when the long-lasting West Yorkshire Coal Owners' Association was formed by 26 colliery concerns in the district (almost all of them being large, with the signal exception of J. & J. Charlesworth), the Briggses were by far the largest producers, with their production for that year amounting to some 735,000 tons, while their next rivals (both topographically and economically), Pope & Pearson at Altofts, produced 475,000 tons. Ten years later - and two years after Snydale Colliery had been taken over - the Briggses produced 1,010,000 tons, and Pope & Pearson (now the third largest, having been overtaken by Lord Masham at Featherstone) produced 513,000 tons. In 1877 the annual Briggs' output had been 590,000 tons.

PLATE V   Whitwood Colliery, Speedwell Yard, c.1870.

DIVERSIFICATION

Henry (Harry) Currer Briggs got his middle name from his paternal grandmother and this name, coupled with Briggs, continued thereafter in his family. He was the elder of his parents surviving sons (the second son, William, having died "*of the croup*" in childhood) and was born at Overton in March 1829. He was christened by the Unitarian minister at Wakefield in May that year, the baptism being registered at Westgate Chapel and at Dr William's Library in London. Like his father, Harry was to have an adventurous business life. He was educated at Worksop and by a private tutor at home, and, at the age of twenty five, he married Catherine, daughter of Edward Shepherd, Master of the West Riding House of Correction at Wakefield (or, in modern parlance, Governor of Wakefield Prison), his father settling £2000 on him. The Shepherds were an interesting family, having been Governors of prisons through four generations, and the new Mrs Briggs's father was a man of reforming tendencies in regard to the office which he held at Wakefield from 1832 to 1865, when he retired. H.C. Briggs went into partnership with his father in 1849, and he and his wife lived with his parents at Outwood Hall after their marriage until 1863 when Briggs moved to Dundee, where a partnership trading as Thompson, Shepherd and Briggs set up as "*large jute spinners*" at the Seafield Works, and the family moved to live at Fernbrae, one of Dundee's mansions. The father-in-law, Edward Shepherd, was responsible for setting up a coco-fibre mat-making manufactory at Wakefield Prison in lieu of the prisoners' previous occupation of oakum-picking (pulling apart old ropes) and he was noted for being concerned with the establishment of industrial homes for ex-prisoners. A manufactory of mats and matting set up at Thornes Wharf in Wakefield was associated with Edward Shepherd's philanthropic interests and run by his son, Walter, and his son-in-law, H.C. Briggs, for a short period until 1862. Early in that year the fine new power loom factory and two small mills forming the Seafield Works in Dundee, owned and run by John Thomson and employing some 2000 hands and manufacturing mats, matting and carpets, closed on the owner's failure, but in the June the business reopened, with Shepherd and Briggs joining Thomson in partnership and taking an active concern in the running of the business. It is possible that the connection between the Wakefield and the Dundee businesses had originated with John Thomson's father's patent of a method of weaving jute carpets and coconut matting, as both works were concerned with those manufactures. Part of the capital required by Harry Briggs was provided by his father, by mortgaging Harry's colliery interest in 1862, and Harry Briggs went to live in Dundee in 1863, Walter Shepherd having preceded him. Like his parents, Briggs was a Unitarian, and he was among the number of English Unitarians recently settled in Dundee who were in part responsible for the revival of the Unitarian cause there in the 1860s. The business in Dundee was continued with Harry Briggs's personal presence until 1869. After Henry Briggs died at Fernbrae (now 329 Perth Road and a nursing home) in 1868, Harry succeeded him as chairman of the Company, an office he retained until his own death. However, Harry Briggs had been managing director of the newly incorporated colliery business at Whitwood from its formation in 1865 until he took over as chairman, and doubtless it was felt essential that he should now return to live in the West Riding. He did so in 1869 and served again as managing director of the Company from 1876 to 1881, which was the period between his brother's leaving Britain and his own death.

Briggs was remembered in Dundee, and an obituary notice in the *Dundee Advertiser*, following his death in Christiana, commented of him that:

> "*Like his father, whom he succeeded in the colliery management, he took very broad enlightened and philanthropic views of public questions, and his influence was always on the side of progress and reform ... He was much disappointed to find that what worked well in prosperous times was not calculated to bear the stress of adverse conditions*".

As though interests in the West Riding and at Dundee were not sufficient in their geographical spread, Harry Briggs and his brother Archibald were intimately involved, both personally and officially, in the rapidly-expanding Cleveland iron industry. This interest almost certainly derived from or through H.K. Spark, who has been mentioned earlier in this monograph. In 1853 ironstone underlying land near Guisborough in Cleveland was leased to Joshua Bates and Thomas Baring - the latter of the celebrated banking firm - for a 63 year term, and in 1861 Spark and his three co-lessees (John Kirsop and Cuthbert and Emerson Muschamp Bainbridge) took some 400 acres of the stone on a sub-lease for 42 years, with power to surrender every seven years. A considerable amount of capital was spent opening mines at South Belmont, with communication by rail with the iron smelting area surrounding Middlesbrough. For example, when the business was bought by the two Briggs brothers in March 1870, they had to pay Spark £15,000 in cash, plus either £10,000's worth of fully paid up stock in any joint-stock company which they might be responsible for forming within twelve months of their purchase, or, if such company was not formed, a similar amount in cash. Spark was to retain the ownership of the ironstone then lying at the mouths of the mines, and he alone seems to have been interested in their actual working. In June 1870 the Briggs brothers agreed to assign their sub-lease to the North of England Company for 3000 shares at £10 each. Production increased markedly in 1873, when over 125,000 tons were drawn, but thereafter fell rapidly to some 35,000 tons in 1875.

Within a few months of their purchase, the Briggs brothers floated a joint stock company to run not only the mines, but also the Carlton Iron Works near Stockton on Tees, which had been established a decade earlier by Samuel Bastow, a Stockton on Tees engineer. He had bought the site in August 1860 for £2000 and turned the business into Samuel Bastow & Co. Ltd, with a capital of £150,000. This firm also owned the Cliff House Iron

Works at West Hartlepool. The Carlton Iron Works were in the township of Whitton and were extensive in their scale, but Bastows had financial troubles and the Briggs brothers bought the works, which then possessed two furnaces, for £13,300 at an auction in March 1870. An insurance valuation of 1874 gives the total costs to that date:

	£
general plant	15,561
blast furnaces	53,408
brickworks	585
malleable iron works	27,489
cottages	7,353
	104,396

plus £5000 which had been spent on extra land. By this time there were three furnaces, each 80 feet in height, one 23½ feet in the bosh and two 18 feet in diameter, and all had been blown in between April 1871 and February 1873. A Danks Patent Puddling Forge with eight furnaces had been built and there was machinery for making boiler plates. The property included a manager's house, six foremen's cottages, 66 other cottages, a Model Lodging House of 45 beds (which cost £835 17s 4d to build) and a public house, called the Carlton Iron Works Inn, which cost £350 to build.

The new company was to be 'The North of England Industrial Iron and Coal Company' and was to have a nominal capital of a £250,000 in £10 shares, with a first call raising £100,000. The revised prospectus, of May 1870, stated that "*The above Company has been formed by Messrs. H. Currer and Archibald Briggs, for the especial purpose of extending to the Iron and Coal trades of the Counties of Durham and North Yorkshire the principle of Industrial partnership, which has worked so advantageously under their management at Whitwood and Methley Collieries, near Normanton.*" Initially the company would produce ironstone and pig iron, but it was planned to extend into the production of coal and to the making of malleable iron and steel, "*for which extension a further issue of shares will be made.*" It was planned to provide easy terms for the purchase of shares by the men and to allow every workman to participate in profits over "*say*" 15 per cent. The prospectus interestingly sets out the advantages of "*Industrial Partnership*", stated to be (in essence) the provision of an initiative for a workman to do his own duty and to see that others did theirs, and the prevention of disputes between masters and men. It would also encourage further care in the use of materials, an interest in the adoption of the most economic and newest methods of working, and the settlement of a good class of workpeople.

The company was successfully floated, with 9975 shares (some third fully paid at £10 and two thirds at £4), bringing in a capital of £60,000. Most of the capital came from persons associated with the Briggs family in the

PLATE VI Archibald Briggs.

Wakefield district or near Dundee. A total of 2646 shares were taken up by the directors of Henry Briggs, Son and Co., with 1486 going to Harry Briggs and 910 to Archibald Briggs, 100 going to Spark, 500 to J.F. Tonge, the Briggs' erstwhile partner at Whitwood, 100 to their Wakefield solicitor, and so forth. Walter Morrison, M.P., the eccentric owner of (and dweller at) Malham Tarn, took up 500 shares and was on the Board. The Comte de Paris had another 500, while the Duc de Chartres had 200. Both the latter were French aristocrats, with the Comte (1838-94) being Pretender to the French throne, while the Duc (1840-1910) was a French prince, and both had considerable interests in the Briggs' sociological experiments.

The profit-sharing features of the business, which are treated at some length in the Board of Trade's 1894 Report on Profit-sharing by Mr D.P. Schloss, came into operation in 1873. Although only a few workmen had then taken shares, a sharing of profits was made as a payment of bonus on wages. From 1874, following the onset of the Great Depression, the business itself became unsuccessful for *"many years"*, and the profit-sharing principle was given up, according to the company, in 1889, as the workmen who were not union members insisted upon striking with the trades unionists when disputes arose - as at Whitwood and Methley Junction collieries. The South Belmont mines ceased to be essential to the company in the mid-1870s and late in 1874 an agreement was made for their transfer to the Weardale Iron Company, which also took their plant at valuation. Meanwhile, ironstone mines had been opened at nearby Ailesbury and a colliery at East Howle. References to the North of England Company in the account books of the Wakefield firm of solicitors who transacted legal business for that concern as well as for the Briggses, continue to August 1875. Some time later the concern changed its title to the Carlton Iron Company.

The financial difficulties of the business had increased during the depression, and mortgages for at least £18,000 were made, while new shares were issued in July 1873 and March 1874. H.C. Briggs had been the first managing

THE NORTH OF ENGLAND

INDUSTRIAL IRON & COAL COMPANY,

(LIMITED.)

DIRECTORS:--

Chairman - - - H. CURRER BRIGGS, Esq.

WALTER MORRISON, ESQ., M.P. | WILLIAM LOWSON, ESQ.

ARCHIBALD BRIGGS, ESQ. | D. RAMSAY RAMSAY, ESQ.

MR. GEORGE LYNAS, Secretary.

REPORT OF DIRECTORS.

The Directors have pleasure in submitting the annexed Statement of Accounts, which includes the whole receipts and expenditure of the Company from the date of its formation to the 30th of April last, covering a period of eleven months. The outlay during that period has been almost exclusively on formation and extension of Works and Plant.

South Belmont Ironstone Mines have been continuously worked during that period, although upon a limited scale; the Directors are, however, glad to be able to report that contracts have recently been entered into, at remunerative rates, which ensure a greatly increased output of ironstone during the current year.

One of the blast furnaces at Carlton Iron Works has recently been brought into successful

Fig.11 The first report of the North of England Company.

director of the new North of England Company, but by 1876 he was back in the West Riding, after what turned out to be a brief residence in Saltburn. By 1881 there were no Briggses on the North of England Company's board and the company had a major debit balance.

The North of England Industrial Iron & Coal Company survived until 1877, when its properties became those of the Carlton Iron Co. Ltd. In due course, coalmining was begun and Mainsforth Colliery was worked. The Carlton Company was reconstructed in 1914, but kept its identity and independence until 1923, when its ironworks at Stillington and its colliery became part of the giant Dorman, Long & Co. Ltd. Walter Morrison remained as chairman of the old concern until at least 1919, when he was well into his eighties, providing a living link with the company's Briggs' days. The works at Stillington closed in 1930 and were dismantled in 1930-31.

It was curious that H.C. Briggs, in particular, should have concerned himself and involved his relatives and partners with the financial and administrative affairs of a highly speculative copper, lead, limestone and freestone extracting concern in the North Riding of Yorkshire at very much the time that the collieries were being expanded and a limited liability company being established for that purpose. However, he seems to have had something of a penchant - or, judging by the outcome in each case, a weakness - for highly speculative ventures, as described below, with the affair of the Merrybent company seeming to have been the greatest of all the failures.

The promotion was concerned with a scheme to open up copper and lead mines at Merrybent, near Melsonby in the North Riding, and to establish a railway to serve both them and the nearby limestone resources, where stone of an average 60 feet thickness and suitable for flux purposes was closer to the Cleveland iron furnaces than any other deposit. The railway was also intended to serve the excellent-quality Gatherley Moor building stone, and there were plans to develop the agricultural countryside along the railway's route. The mines, quarries and railway were all promoted in the 1860s. The mines, in an area where copper had been successfully worked in the 18th century, were run privately from 1862 until a joint stock company was established in July 1864 as the Merrybent & Middleton Tyas Mining & Smelting Co. Ltd, with over £21,000 being paid for the Merrybent estate of some 344 acres. The initial investment was as follows:

	£
Merrybent estate	21,200
additional land, 12 acres	8,000
copper & lead ore leases, lease of limestone	
for 46 years, cost of mining plant, some	25,000
railway Act and deposit	6,000
plant and labour	10,000
preliminary expenses	300
	54,500

The new company included both Henry and Harry Briggs among its shareholders, and Harry became one of its first directors, soliciting relatives, friends and acquaintances to invest in the concern. In June 1866 powers were obtained to build a six and a half mile long railway from the vicinity of the mines and quarries to join the North Eastern Railway's system. Its capital of £50,000 was held in trust by the mining company, which itself contributed between £20,000 and £25,000 towards the railway's cost. The company was then reconstructed, as the New Merrybent Company, with

Harry Briggs retaining a seat on the board. The new company was still seriously undercapitalised, however, and borrowed money, rather than raising it by the issue of additional shares. In 1865 £10,000 was borrowed at 4 per cent. Three years later, this was replaced by £8000 borrowed from Edward Tew, the Wakefield banker, at 4½ per cent. This loan was still outstanding in 1876. Debentures had to be issued at a substantial 6 per cent between 1871 and 1873, to a total value of almost £14,000, substantial parts of that sum being provided by Harry and Archie Briggs, and by their partners, the Tonges.

Initial prospects had looked good and, in 1865, Harry Briggs had written that *"I and my Father mean to take as many shares as we can manage, probably 1000"* (of £10 paid). Harry soon complained of the inertia of others of his co-directors, however, and in October 1866 he wrote to his lawyer, P.C. Skipworth of Wakefield (who addresses him as *"Dear Currer"*), wishing that in hindsight Skipworth had bought colliery - Briggses' - shares, rather than mining ones. The lead and copper mines shewed some initial promise, with production to May 1868 being upwards of £7000's worth of lead and copper ores. John Tattersall, just appointed manager and being a shareholder in the concern and who was also the most experienced *"miner in Swaledale"* where fine success had recently been achieved at the Keld Head and Old Gang mines, reported well.

Spark joined the board of the new company and in 1868 he gained effective control and became chairman. Work was pushed ahead with the long-delayed railway, where an earlier decision had been reached to lay the line with light 65 lbs rails which would save money but only allow use by goods traffic. In August 1868 Briggs wrote that an advertisement had been placed in the *Leeds Mercury* newspaper for sub-contractors for the masonry on some two miles of the line. It was Spark who opened the line in June 1870 and he who, in November 1870, advanced £10,000 on mortgage of the company's estates. Harry Briggs retained his directorship and became chairman in 1871 when Spark was ousted in a boardroom coup. A counter-coup in 1872 led to Spark's return, however, and Briggs resigned from the board in February of that year, subsequently selling his shares and disassociating himself from the concern. Briggs may indeed have sold well, for in October 1874 a petition was made for the winding up of the company. Spark became a bankrupt in consequence in 1876 and the mine was disposed of and its plant sold by auction in June 1878, although the railway continued to work until 1950. The amount of ores sold was never especially remarkable, but the limestone production was to remain significant for many decades. This was an apparently sorry episode for Harry Briggs, although his reputation seems not to have suffered in any way from his connection with it. Briggs himself claimed that he had been brought into the concern through the interests of its promoters, Messrs Bradley, father and son. He also claimed that he had *"spent a great deal of time & money over the affair"*.

Harry Briggs also had extensive interests outside the collieries and his iron, copper and railway concerns in North Yorkshire. He was joint owner of some iron-works, described as extensive, in Brazil and he was concerned in the Apedale lead mines, in Wensleydale. He was also involved in a patent process which successfully produced paving slabs from cement and Shap granite, and in copper and silver mines at Bratsbeg in Norway, while in Cornwall he had an interest in the Wheal Agar Mine, a copper and tin mine run on the cost-book system. This mine was one of those which, in 1897, were absorbed within the famous East Pool Mine as the East Pool & Agar United Mines. His interests were, however, required more and more at Whitwood after 1876, with his brother's retirement from an active position in the colliery business. He moved to Harrogate in 1873 and to Leeds in 1876 and was probably able to give more time to the colliery business then, because, as Clara Clarkson commented in her diary in the latter year (repeating the latest gossip from Mr Barmby, who was her minister and Harry's brother-in-law), *"the Iron Works of the Briggs' at Middlesbro' have not paid a farthing to the shareholders and it is rumoured they are about to fail"*. Harry Briggs died suddenly and unexpectedly in October 1881, while visiting the mines at Bratsberg. He had fallen while on the ship, and this and his gout had made him very lame, but death was not anticipated, at least by Briggs himself. He had commented to his wife less than a week before his death that *"This mine is grand and is now making £200 profit per month"*.

H.C. Briggs was perhaps the real founder of the success of the colliery company, and certainly the founder of the co-partnership as well as the incorporation scheme. He had been able to write as early as August 1868 that the Whitwood (etc) report and balance sheet *"is most satisfactory. Everyone is pleased except that cantankerous uncle of mine Mr Wm Briggs - I have had a deal of bother with him he tries to pick holes in every thing"*, even though the shares, £10 paid, were then selling in Wakefield at £15. A few months earlier in October 1866, he had written that the colliery *"has been a most wonderful success ..."*. At his death, Harry Briggs had property worth £47,337 10s 5d.

Archibald Briggs, the younger surviving son of Henry, was born in January 1833. In 1860, immediately prior to his marriage, he was described as of Liverpool, merchant. There he attended Renshaw Street Chapel (Unitarian), and he was a member of its Home Mission Committee in 1855, subsequently delivering a free lecture on life in the coal pits, and later a course on physical geography. His marriage to Miss Alice Sophia Steward, daughter of James Steward of Llandudno, took place in Llandudno in September 1860 and Archibald received a marriage portion of £3000 from his father. For some time then, Archibald and his wife lived with the Henry and Harry Briggses, *en famille*, at Outwood Hall, but in 1866 they leased the nearby Moor House in Stanley cum Wrenthorpe township and they remained there until 1872, when a seven-year repairing lease of Stanley Hall was taken. This property included the mansion with its entrance lodge and some six-and-three-quarter acres of grounds, with a house on the opposite side of the adjoining Aberford turnpike road. The house was taken fully furnished, at £187 a year with a further £85 for the furnishings, with the curious provision that not only were three rooms reserved by the owner, but that he retained the right to occupy the house for three month periods between June 1st and November 11th in any of the lease years 1874,1876 or 1877. Briggs took the flowers (listed) in two greenhouses and outside in the gardens, and the garden tools, and he spent a substantial £523 15s 9d on making the house comfortable, though only £100 of this was allowed by the owner. The tenancy was retained until 1879, when numbers of the books in the library of the house and various other items were missing and had to be paid for, together with £75 in dilapidations.

Meanwhile, on the formation of the new colliery company in 1865, Archibald Briggs became its first secretary and ultimately succeeded his brother as managing director (Harry Briggs then being chairman) during the years 1869-76. In 1873 he was receiving £1,000 a year in this capacity. The couple had two sons and three daughters, but, when his wife's health broke down, Briggs gave up his position with the colliery, although he remained a director until 1880. The family then lived abroad, first in Algiers where he had owned property since at least 1866, and later in various parts of Italy. Early in 1875 he became a partner in a coffee plantation in Ceylon and in August 1876 Clara Clarkson wrote in her diary that Mr and Mrs Briggs *"are leaving Stanley Hall and this district for good. An uncle of Mr Briggs's has left him a cork forest in Pernambuco and they think living in a warmer climate will be a help to Mrs Briggs who has a consumptive tendency."* Archibald was reported as having been an active Unitarian and a prominent member of Westgate Chapel, where he had paid pew rent up to the end of the Lady Day quarter in 1879, and he had taken the chair at a number of annual meetings of the West Riding Unitarian Mission. He was an acquaintance of the Emperor of Brazil, having met him when visiting that country, and it was he who invited the Emperor to visit the collieries at Whitwood, as he did in 1871. Archibald lived on for a decade after leaving Wakefield, though in deteriorating health. In January 1880 he was recovering from an illness and in March 1880 he was in Florence, awaiting an operation for an abscess on the liver. While fishing alone on Lake Garda in 1886, Briggs drowned at the age of 53, an event reported in the Wakefield Liberal paper in July of that year. In his will of March 1873, when living at Stanley Hall, Briggs refers to his own 400 shares in Henry Briggs, Son & Company, and his 300 shares in the North of England Industrial Company, and to his business in shipping, ironwork, machinery and other (unspecified) articles and to Pernambuco. He appointed his brother and his wife as his executors, but left personal estate valued at only £4691 2s 11d. In personality, Briggs was described as *"highly intellectual, but nevertheless modest in his habits"*. His two sons were to take no part in the management of the business, even though the elder of them was nineteen at his father's death.

The brains behind the latter 19th and early 20th century prosperity of the Company were those of A.C. Briggs and his brother-in-law, Walter Geoffrey Jackson - a Briggs, so to speak, by marriage. Jackson was born in November 1846 at Malton, the second son of middle class parents. As a young man he followed an engineering appointment in Bolton, then worked from 1867 to 1872 for the Argentine Great Southern Railway, before returning home in his mid-20s to work in engineering and coalmining on Teesside in the North Riding of Yorkshire. He was elected to membership of the North of England Institute of Mining & Mechanical Engineers in June 1873, when he lived in Saltburn. That town was the home of A.C. Briggs and his family, and Jackson married Briggs' only daughter in 1877. Jackson was appointed engineer to the collieries of which his father-in-law was managing director, and he came to live in Methley, moving to Loscoe Grange after the company bought the Holdsworth estate there in 1881. In 1879 he took an articled pupil, the son of George Robson, as colliery manager. Jackson was appointed a director in November 1880, when he was still only in his early thirties. Upon H.C. Briggs's unexpected death in 1881, Richard Tonge took over the chairmanship and the young A.C. Briggs took over as managing director. Jackson was appointed as certificated manager of the collieries, and for some time he was agent, too. With his wife and daughter, Jackson moved to live at Hicklam House at Aberford, from where he travelled to the collieries which he and Arthur Briggs ran so successfully until 1896, when, at the age of 50, he retired from active management owing to ill health, but remained a director of the company. The family moved to live at Bramham Hall, but he also owned an estate of some 200 acres in the parish of Chiddingford in Surrey (to which he was ultimately to retire). He was a member of the Leeds Club and enjoyed the recreations of fishing and shooting.

Jackson's retirement was broken in 1906 when, following the death of his brother-in-law, his fellow directors requested his recall to become chairman and managing director. He remained as managing director until 1919 and as chairman until 1924, when, at the age of about 80, he was succeeded by Dr Walter Hargreaves, Li.D. Jackson remained a director, however, and was also a director of the Briggs Trust Company, the Whitwood Chemical Company, the Yorkshire Electric Power Company, and the Wressle Boring Company, as well as being a Member of the Royal Society of Arts and the Institute of Mining Engineers. He died in May 1936, when he was 89 years old. A *Yorkshire Post* obituary refers to his vast knowledge of engineering and of the coal industry, his *"love of fair dealing"* and his ardent advocacy of mutual trust and co-operation with the workpeople. He had lived latterly at Prestwick, Chiddingford, Godalming, and he left estate of the gross value of £171,754. Curiously, there was no obituary of Jackson in the subsequent issue of the *Wakefield Express* newspaper, then as now circulating in Normanton.

INNOVATION IN TECHNOLOGY AND ADMINISTRATION

Writing in 1862, Parkin Jeffcock, the mining engineer, commented that "*the 'long wall' system* [of coal working] *is being extended in the Yorkshire coalfield; and wherever it can be adopted it is to be recommended on account of the simplicity of arrangement both for working and ventilation, and as being the most economical method of getting the coal.*"

He goes on to report that the system used at Flockton, where, at least in 1849, the system of working the coal had been similar to that used at Whitwood, seems to be the "*Bank Work*" method, in which the coal was got in banks some 60 yards long without any intermediate pillars, as they became liable to heavy pressure, rendering the coal in them of little value. Jeffcock says that the bords or working roadways in "*Yorkshire bank work*" were cut against the face of the coal, transversely to its grain and following the rise of the coal, with a series of endings at right angles into the intervening coal which was then worked out, to leave only sufficient coal on each side of the bords to support the roof over them and to allow hence for getting coal out and maintaining ventilation.

The layout of any colliery obviously depended largely on the original area(s) of coal leased and on how the shafts were located and the underground workings laid out. The location of the successive shafts at Whitwood was on the upward end (the rise) of the coal, which was unusual - as it was usual to locate shafts at the downward end or dip, to allow water drainage.

By 1882, much unsaleable coal, presumably from the coal washery, was being produced by the Briggses, who then asked Lord Mexborough's agent about building a coking plant and using gas from it to fire the colliery's boilers. The agent, however, held out no hope of such an agreement being made, and the Briggses went ahead with work on non-Mexborough land to develop the chemical works and by-product plant at Normanton Common, under a separate company and jointly with another concern.

As with so many of the other larger coalmasters in the early 1870s, the Briggses were much interested in the possibility of mechanical coal-cutting by the use of undercutting machines. Rising wages, and hence costs, in a period of massive competition had encouraged both the invention and the adoption of such machines. In 1863 a number of local coalmasters, representing Foxholes and Altofts collieries, both adjoining the Briggses' royalty, and Kippax colliery, whose owner later in the decade developed St John's colliery at Newland, which also adjoined the Briggses' royalty, had been to see a Firth type of coal cutter at work at West Ardsley, although none of the Briggses went with them. Two years previously, the most successful of the early machines used regionally was patented by Donisthorpe, Firth & Ridley, the two former of whom were partners in a colliery at West Ardsley, where their machines were first used, powered by compressed air, but in August 1863 the Briggses settled with a Ridley & Jones machine, which had been patented only a couple of months earlier. The situation was so complex, however, as rival inventors claimed the partial use of their own patented improvements by others, that the Briggses found it desirable to be indemnified against any legal actions which might be started against them. In this instance, Firth & Donisthorpe were making claims upon the ideas utilised by Ridley & Jones. Robert Ridley was a local man, living at Beeston Hill, while J.G. Jones was from Pentonville. Both were engineers by occupation.

What is significant is that by the end of 1863 the Briggses had *"seen all the [coal-cutting] Machines in existence in this Country"*. An article in *The Colliery Guardian* had commended the Ridley & Jones machine, although as late as December 1863 those partners had not had their patent specification printed. It seems likely that at least one machine of this type was used by the Briggses, but, doubtlessly, as with other machines in this field, it proved impracticable and probably uneconomic, too. In 1869 a Firth machine was in use at the nearby West Riding Colliery at Altofts, and a fresh outburst of enthusiasm for machine-undercutting was evinced. Sharlston Colliery, also quite close to Altofts, bought machines which were paid for in 1872, while a year earlier Bradley & Craven, the engineers of Wakefield, had built an air-compressor for working a coal cutter at Woolley Colliery. In 1870 the Briggses were negotiating for an undercutting machine, which, according to the price list, would cost £56 10s 0d. It was to be provided by one Frederick Hurd, previously of Rochdale but since March 1870 of the Albion Foundry in Alverthorpe Road, Wakefield. Hurd claimed to be sole grantee of a patent registered in March 1870, a half share in which he had sold to William Firth for £3,000. A Mr Pilling also wished to sell coal-cutting machines to the Company, and his were somewhat cheaper than Hurd's. However, Hurd claimed that he, and not his erstwhile business partner Pilling, was the owner of the patent. A search was made at the Patent Office and the situation elucidated. In reality, the Hurd machine had also been patented in France and Belgium, and an application for a patent had been made in the USA.

It is not clear whether Hurd machines - or any other mechanical coalcutters - were introduced at this time or not, but certainly the onset of the depression in 1874 put an end to their use throughout the whole region. Hurd's original machine worked cutters attached to a chain, but in the 1870s he took up the idea of a disc machine and ultimately moved to favour a third type. This was a bar machine, whose form he improved and gave the general arrangement, which it still possesses. Coal-cutting machines seem to have been used only marginally in even the larger West Riding collieries until the 1890s, but Pope & Pearson's West Riding colliery at Altofts, near Normanton, was one which tried them frequently - in 1869, 1882, and c.1888 - and used them regularly from c.1892 in the form of the Diamond machine.

Naturally only a part of the real story of the various Briggs' collieries and their day-to-day life can be recovered at this distance of time, and then it is the extra-ordinary rather than the ordinary which is illustrated by the surviving documentation. But some details of colliery life do survive, especially where its formal rules had been transgressed.

In 1871, an explosion at the Good Hope pit burnt two men. At the time, the barometer was low and the presence of gas anticipated, so that the men were ordered to work with safety lamps. Boards marked "fire" were erected to guard against men passing danger points with naked lights, but some did. In November 1881 two men among twenty who lived in Castleford brought a lawsuit against the company. One said that he could not make a living working where he did, and he wanted an allowance or a better job. The Bottom Steward went to see the workplace complained of, but the men had already left their work and they subsequently claimed the 1s 7d which the company always made a new workman deposit when engaged, to cover the cost of the tools used. They had contracted to work as stallmen, and hence they had broken their own contracts.

At the Silkstone pit at Whitwood at this period, average earnings were 4s 5½d a day, and the average week worked was one of 5½ days. The men were paid at 1s 7d a ton. In September 1874 printed forms were issued to determine the current hiring on October 9th 1874. Wages and prices were to be reduced by 10 per cent and the men informed "*that if your services be continued it must be on those terms.*" At Whitsuntide in 1874 the men ceased work on the Saturday and resumed on the Wednesday. Somewhat earlier, in 1857, a question had arisen as to how far the printed and issued colliery byelaws were binding on the colliers. The clerk to the magistrates was himself uncertain on the point and sought the opinion of counsel. One case against a collier was in fact dismissed on the grounds that a man had not received a copy of the rules, and another case withdrawn against five men who had left the company's service owing, as the lawyer politely put it in his bill for the business, to "*an informality in your Byelaws*". In consequence, new byelaws were made in 1857. In 1858 a strike was anticipated, resulting from a reduction in wages. Eight ringleaders were summonsed, and they agreed to pay the costs of the case against them and return to work. This quick action seems to have forestalled the strike.

In 1862 David Frudd, formerly a chimney sweep and latterly a collier for the Briggses, was allowed to leave their service without formal notice on becoming the men's checkweighman. G.H. Scholefield was the Company's weighman and the two checked the corves together. Two or three times a day a corf would be sent back for reweighing, and on one occasion Frudd attacked Scholefield and was given notice by George Robson, the top-manager. Frudd, who lived at Cleggs Buildings in Castleford, sued the Company for £2 14s 0d, but the verdict went for the Briggses. In the same year, Thomas Kitchen and his father came to work for the partners, the lad becoming one of a group hurrying in the pit in groups of four or six and who were paid as a gang at 10d per dozen corves. Thomas was weakly, however, and could not push uphill, so he received a little less when the gang was paid weekly on Saturdays in small change, which they divided among themselves at the Robin Hood public house. Reference is made at this time to a day shift, suggesting that a night shift existed, too. The boy Kitchen's father was paid 1s 10d "*by the piece*" for each ton of coal he got which was sent to bank, and the usual rate for men of his type was 4s 6d a day. Kitchen agitated for a strike at a men's meeting at one Pickersgill's public house, but there was no seconder to a motion to demand an increase. He was warned by the management about trouble-making, was abusive and left. The byelaws stated that two weeks' notice on either side was required. In practice, however, none was usual, but here a minor lawsuit arose. Thomas Kitchen senior had come from Lancashire. He had "*laked*" for twelve months at the expense of the Union. His tools were his own.

The Company ran what was in fact a good, safe colliery, a situation in part owed to their care and in part to the largely non-gaseous nature of the seams worked. The numbers of pit fatalities were (relatively) low, as the following table shews. The figures are compared with those of the Coal Kings, J. & J. Charlesworth.

	Briggs	Charlesworth		Briggs	Charlesworth
1868	1	6	1879	5	2
1869	0	2	1880	2	2
1870	2	0	1881	4	1
1871	0	4	1882	2	3
1872	2	2	1883	1	2
1873	6	5	1884	2	2
1874	3	26	1885	3	2
1875	10	3	1886	5	1
1876	1	2	1887	1	2
1877	4	1	1888	1	5
1878	1	5		56	78

The failure of the co-partnership scheme in the mid 1880s was immediately followed by a sharp rise in Union membership, as the following Yorkshire Miners' Association figures, of contributions as subscriptions, demonstrate:-

	1885	1890
	£	£
Whitwood Mere (sic)	30	468
Methley	36	313
Good Hope	167	336

The numbers of strikes increased too, many being but local ones and those often occasioned by relatively minor irritations. In November 1882 some

500 men struck at Don Pedro and Good Hope pits, as the price of house coal was increased and the men were angry over the company's compulsory but (to them) unnecessary use of lamps underground. A meeting of the men was held in the Bicycle Hall at Normanton Common, with Hugh Bryne, a checkweighman at Good Hope pit, in the chair. At this time, some Don Pedro men were paid as little as 2s 9d a day for five days a week, but the men at the different pits belonging to the Company were disunited. *"For a long time"* there had been a joint committee of men from all the pits, but after Mr Maskrey had left, *"the committee seemed to collapse"*. Case papers appertaining to these proceedings in 1884 contain a list of 203 men employed at Don Pedro pit, with the addresses of most. They nearly all lived close to the colliery, with only a handful from as far away as Cutsyke and the furthest being from Castleford.

Some details of the actual working of the colliery in the 1850s emerge from a study of the regulations printed for use by the workmen and officials of the concern in 1856 and again in 1861, as provided for in the Coal Mines Inspection Act of 1856. They were formulated for the approval of Charles Morton, by then the regional Inspector of Mines, and were printed by the Briggses' co-Unitarian, George Horridge of Wakefield. The general and special rules of 1856 were *"to be observed by the Owners, Agent, Under-Viewer, Deputies, and Work-People of Henry Briggs and Son's Whitwood & Fairies' Hill Collieries, near Normanton"* and covered ventilation, the fencing of air-shafts, disused shafts and working pits when in use, the lining of, and signalling in, shafts, the use of a shaft depth indicator and a proper brake by the engineman, together with steam boiler gauges and safety valves. They went on to detail the responsibilities of enginemen, banksmen and hangers-on, of (ventilation) furnace men, of enginemen and brakesmen on inclined planes, of locomotive enginemen and stokers, as well as those of the agent, under viewer, deputies and miners. These rules largely followed a regional pattern, but the byelaws which were printed at their end were specific to the Whitwood collieries and are worth abstracting:

   – a fortnight's notice was to be given by each side

   – each workman was to be given a copy of the rules and pay 3d if lost

   – miners "are expected to produce as much large coal as the nature of the mine will admit", free of rubbish, and if a corf was sent to bank not well filled or with rubbish, it would be lost to the workman/men

   – hours of work for carpenters, blacksmiths, sawyers, wood-cutters, mechanics, pick-sharpeners, bricklayers, masons, coke burners, coal pickers and labourers were 6am to 5pm, and on Saturdays to 4 pm, meal times being 8-8.30, 12-12.30

PLATE VII   Methley Junction Colliery (Henry Briggs, Son & Co.) c.1870.

– the men were to pay 2d each and boys 1d towards the Accident Fund, from which 7s to men and 3s 6d to boys per week would be paid in case of accident, and medical aid provided.   The men were to appoint two of their number to audit these accounts twice yearly

– the loss or destruction of tools would be charged to each man - a shovel 3s, hammer 2s, a tomahawk 2s, a pick 1s 6d, a wedge 3d, a tool shaft 2d, a riddle 1s 6d, a safety lamp 7s, a dog and chain 2s 6d, a buffet 2d.

– a system of fines for colliery offences was set out for the sole purpose of ensuring the safety and comfort of the workmen and the protection of the colliery and all fines were to be paid to the Accident fund.

These byelaws were similar to those agreed for the collieries of Milnes, Stansfeld & Co, in which until lately Henry Briggs had had a partner's interest, but the latter rules interestingly specify labourers' hours as 6 a.m. to 5.30 p.m. (5 p.m. on Saturdays) with 1½ hours of breaks, while colliers' hours are laid down as 6.30 a.m. to 2 p.m., with no collier taking more than one day's holiday in each fortnight.   Further rules, now for the Methley Junction and Whitwood Collieries, were dated in April 1861.   They allude to the use of naked lights, to the working of incline ropes or chains in shafts, to a maximum of four persons travelling together in the shaft, to injured being taken to the Infirmary (at Leeds) and to wages being paid in money and at the Pay Office.

The discipline necessarily maintained in the working of the colliery was supported by successive Inspectors of Mines and their staffs, and the Inspectors' own powers were increased during this period. In 1884, the Inspector had insisted that shotfiring should only take place when the mine was clear of its colliers. Boys driving horses underground rode on the corve shafts and were liable to considerable hurt. Some boys were lamed, the others warned, and two caught riding on the shafts were brought before the magistrates, although the Company's solicitors were instructed not "*to press the case*". In 1902 boys at both Methley and Savile were prosecuted for riding horses on the travelling roads underground. In 1897 a byeworkman, James Lord, was working on the construction of a new engine plane extension at Savile Colliery. His work was poor, but he refused to transfer to the coal face and was dismissed. The undermanager at Savile at the time, Joseph Hough, had been in the Company's employ for 30 years and more.

At Savile again, in 1898, a stand-in onsetter gave the signal to raise the cage before the full tubs were secured. This caused some damage to equipment and the pit stopped for 45 minutes, with the loss of 40 tons of coal. Again in 1898, but at Snydale, a 19 year old Normanton lad, who had been a pony driver successively at Don Pedro, Sharlston, Newland St John's and Snydale for six or seven years, was prosecuted for having brought a run of three tubs from faces in the Western District of the Haigh Moor workings to the passbye and there having failed to secure them, whereby they moved and the pony was run over and killed. In 1894 a quite different offence was recorded, when a man clandestinely exchanged the motties, which shewed who had produced the contents of which tub and thus controlled wage payments, on the tubs. Another offence was largely the result of women and children searching on the spoil heaps for burnable coal. In 1902 there was something of a crackdown on this practice, which was never encouraged, after the long roadside tip at Snydale was picked over and, as a result, collapsed into the ditch which separated it from the highway.

In the West Yorkshire coalfield, output per man year rose from 262 tons in 1901, the year of the first reliable figures, to 275 tons in 1913, and under the Minimum Wage Act of 1912, a regional minimum wage of 3s 7d a day (plus the regional percentage) was agreed. Much technical improvement was then occurring in coal-getting technology, and mechanical coalcutters were first successfully used by the Briggses in 1888, following the success of the Bower, Blackburn & Mori electrically-driven machine. The objective of coalcutting was, as it had been with the early attempts, to reduce costs, as machine mining allowed the concentration of the area worked with a larger output from a given area and thus needing shorter underground roadways, simpler ventilation and improved supervision. In 1902 only 483 cutting machines were in use in the whole country, nearly one third of which used electricity and the rest compressed-air. These cutters got only 1.8 per cent of all coal output. By 1916 this percentage had risen to over 10, with 3459 machines, and it topped 15 by 1922, with 5434 machines in use. The Briggses gradually introduced more and more machine cutting, soon going over to coalcutters of the disc, chain and bar types, which were worked by compressed-air and made a six foot undercut. Coal was usually cut by machine end-on to its grain, but hand cutting was done at 45 degrees to the cleat. In a few faces it was cut on bord. Gates were 33 or 44 yards apart.

Detail of the internal administration of the collieries derives from the printed rules made under the Coal Mines Acts of 1887 to 1896. In their detail, the General Rules follow the provisions of the appropriate national legislation, while the Special Rules, the Form of Contract, the Byelaws and the List of prices of miners' tools are special to their own collieries. The new Special Rules were arranged according to the duties of individual officers, in line of hierarchical descent, and they illustrate the point that an internal reorganisation of the collieries had occurred since 1861:

1861	c1896
Agent	Manager
Underground Viewer	Under Manager
deputy underground viewer	Under Viewer
engine man	deputies
banksman and assistant	engine wright
hangers-on	engine men
furnacemen	banksman
lamp keepers	hangers-on
doorkeepers	underground enginemen
underground enginemen	underground brakesmen
underground brakesmen	underground incline
underground train boys	underground train boys
on self-acting inclines	on inclines
	furnace men
	lamp keepers / head lampkeeper
	doorkeepers
	horsekeepers
	drivers
	miners
	hurriers or trammers.

R.T. Shaw, MIMinE, some time manager at Whitwood, wrote an interesting paper - which was published - on *The Making of a Colliery Price List*, and this important subject - an agreement for paying the colliers and other underground faceworkers - is of particular significance and historical fascination. The standard textbook on coalmining, Bulman and Redmayne's *Colliery Working and Management*, published in many editions from 1896 and still current between the World Wars, had pointed out that *"the successful working of a Colliery implies the getting of the largest proportion of the workable coal in the best condition, at the lowest possible cost, and with the greatest safety and comfort to those employed"*. A Price List was a major contributor to such success, as it should contain a clear statement of the method of working the coal, and of the other associated duties, including the setting and drawing out of timber, building chocks and packs, laying and pulling up rails, shifting forward of flat sheets (for tubs beyond the rails), all of which were done in this locality by the collier and his assistant. An unclear statement in the Price List could well lead to a trade dispute or even a strike. Shaw in his paper gives some practical advice:

"Having drawn up this Price List in such a way that it clearly states the manner in which it is intended to work the coal, we next come to the all important question of the fixing of the prices. By this shall all men know whether he is a manager in deed as well as in name. He must get such a price as will enable him to compete on level terms with his neighbours but it must be sufficiently generous to attract the best class of workmen.

There is no task more difficult than to manage a colliery where the price paid for the work done is such that the average workman cannot get a reasonable wage. The best class of men will not work there, only those stay who cannot find employment elsewhere, methods degenerate, the minimum wage list increases, output goes down, whilst costs go up and the end is trouble.

It should be remembered that, if the possible wage earned by the collier is not considerably higher than the amount fixed as the minimum wage, there is always the very strong probability that the workman in the moderate place will do as little as possible and fall back on to the minimum rather than put forth the extra exertion which would be necessary to get him very little more.

Nevertheless things being as they are, we all know that it is much easier to get a price fixed that is too high than too low, and I would give you one golden rule; always fix your prices on the result of piece work trials and never on those obtained by day work. It seems almost an impossibility to get anything like fair results from men working at the coal face who are paid by the day.

Care should be taken during the trial period that the number of men do not become excessive as the strictest supervision is necessary. Be sure that the organisation of the transport is thoroughly perfect during the trial time, as indeed it should be at all times. Nothing is worse and more mortifying than to get bad results during the trial period because men have not got their work out."

In November 1904, the Briggses agreed new prices with their colliers at the Whitwood Silkstone Colliery. For working coal by hand undercutting, where the coal was above or below 3 feet 4 inches thick, prices for all coal-getting and associated work and for bringing the coal into the main underground roadway were 1s 8d and 1s 11d per ton respectively, with up to 2s 4d per ton where the Hard Coal and the Gas Coal both occurred, plus extra prices for ripping and packing at so much per foot thickness. Where coal was undercut by coal-cutting machines (to a depth of five feet), the prices ranged upwards from 1s 0d per ton, according to the Price List of August 1903. Hand getting was on the butty system, whereby a self-employed team worked a particular area, in 1904. All prices were subject to the rise and fall of the West Yorkshire District percentage on top of wage payments on the basis of the wage rates of 1888. The excess was 47¼ per cent in August 1903 and 37¼ per cent in November 1904, both of which may be compared with the 50 per cent and 40 per cent agreed regionally.

PLATE VIII   Whitwood Colliery, Speedwell Yard, c.1900.

COAL MARKETS AND USES

The firm's decision to extend and regulate exports of their coal led to the establishment of a subordinate company, called the Yorkshire Coal & Steam Ship Company, Ltd, in 1873. Alexander Meek, a recently established coal merchant at Goole, agreed in 1871 to sell only Briggs' coal, at a commission of 2d a ton, in the town and port of Goole, and in January 1873 he and Archibald Briggs, together with J.S Bailey of Methley, joined in partnership in the steamship *Whitwood* and in the lease of 50 eight ton, standard gauge coal waggons, hired from the Railway Rolling Stock Co. Ltd. A prospectus was issued during 1873 for the establishment of the Yorkshire Coal & Steam Ship Co. Ltd, with a capital of £75,000 in £5 shares, which would buy out Alexander Meek & Partners as steamship owners for £11,250 in shares, and Meek's own coal exporting business for £1000. It was proposed to build another steamer, to carry some 600 tons and to extend the "*already valuable connection*" with Henry Briggs, Son & Company. In fact, a different method of financing was arranged, with the goodwill of the business, the ship and the lease of the waggons being assigned to Briggses in return for 500 'A' shares in their company, while the Briggses held shares numbers 1 to 350 inclusive in the Steam Ship Company, with A.C. Briggs as the managing director. Meek agreed to become the new company's manager for five years, entering into a bond in £2000 for his honesty, and sold his own coal and coke exporting and dealing business to the company as from January 1st 1874. The Yorkshire Company's vessels were specially built and strengthened in the bows to withstand the ice and rough weather on the Hamburg and Baltic routes, but it still suffered an early disaster with the grounding and subsequent wrecking of its fine new screw steamship *The Stanley Main*, built by the Goole Engineering & Shipbuilding Company. A court of inquiry held in 1876 found that the ship's master had been reckless, and suspended his licence for six months.

At Goole, the Yorkshire Company had its rivals. The Goole Shipping Co. Ltd had been established in 1864 and owned a considerable fleet, while the Humber Steam Shipping Co. also had a small fleet. The two minor companies, the Yorkshire and the Humber, were both absorbed by the Goole Co. in the 1890s, when the Briggs' market was well secured. The Goole Company itself was bought out by the Lancashire & Yorkshire Railway under its Act of August 1904. Latterly, the Yorkshire Company had seven vessels, built between 1877 and 1891 and of gross tonnages of from 750 to 1420. Two of these vessels survived until the 1930s. The Lancashire & Yorkshire Railway's sea trade from Goole was largely with Northern Europe, and that probably mirrors the principal markets served by Briggs' coals. Large quantities of coal were ultimately exported from Hull, too, and as the depression eased finally, the amounts of coal exported from Hull increased vastly. To the nearest 1000 tons, the Briggs' figures were as follows:-

	1911	1912	1913
Methley Savile	0	1,000	2,000
Snydale	2,000	5,000	8,000
Water Haigh	0	1,000	6,000
Whitwood	86,000	125,000	177,000
	88,000	132,000	193,000

The Briggs' company also had a number of river vessels of its own. The exact number is not known, but in 1870 ropes were bought from a Knottingley ropemaker for a vessel which was also repaired by John Cliffe, a Knottingley timber merchant and ship builder. Local sales continued, by road, water and rail. In 1892 a coal salesman employed by the Company was found guilty of embezzlement in regard to landsales from Good Hope pit and he was sentenced to two months' hard labour. To what extent the Company supplied other markets is unknown at present, although such was done, as, for example, in the 1860s coal went to Amsterdam.

The process of selling coal to the best financial advantage, through its sale in the largest possible quantities in the most numerous and widely spread of markets, was one which received the careful attention of the Briggs' partners. Such pre-1859 documentation as survives to illustrate this matter suggests the use of three processes. The first was by customers ordering coal direct from the colliery. The second, as in the case of many other larger collieries of the district, was by customers, including distant coal merchants, who were called upon for orders at the same time as a round of collecting payments was being made, and the third was by boatmen who bought coal at the colliery staiths and went off to sell it as best they could. An example of the first seems to lie in the well-documented sales to the glassworks of George Bradley, the Castleford lawyer and speculator, in the 1850s. Although the distance from the colliery to the glassworks in Castleford was small, being some mile or so, the coal was carried in railway waggons on the main line, and numbers of both Briggs' accounts and the waggon consignment labels which were used, survive among Bradley's papers.

Little is known of the Briggs' collieries in the 1840s, and only the surface works are shewn on three maps of the period, which are the 1/10560 Ordnance Survey sheet of 1838-40, the tithe award map of Whitwood and the 1/10560 Ordnance Survey, surveyed in 1846-48. A solitary account has survived in the writer's collection, headed "Whitwood Colliery, near Wakefield", shewing that Henry Briggs, alone, was between January and June 1849 supplying coal graded as best, seconds, riddled and unriddled slack, and smudge. Billheads of the 1850s shew Henry Briggs selling best and lime or engine coals and riddled and unriddled slack. Those used in 1860 and 1861 among the author's Adam Jessop MSS are still headed "Fairies' Hill Colliery, near Normanton" and shew the coals as best, seconds, best nuts, which are all Haigh Moor seam coals, and unriddled slack.

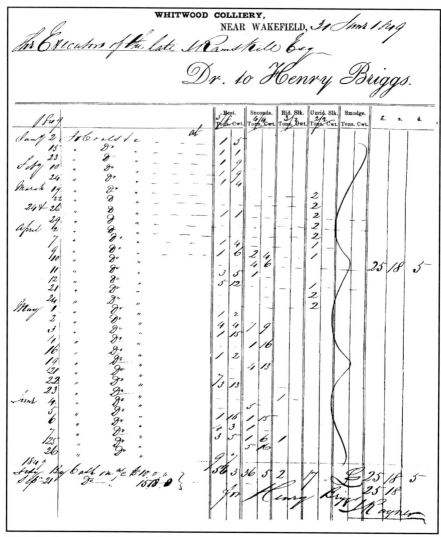

Fig.12 An early Henry Briggs coal account, 1849.

The Aire & Calder Navigation's records of coal shipments, which cover the years 1851-70, indicate quite small shipments by water from Whitwood in the earlier part of that period, rising in the later 1860s, presumably as continental markets developed, and they were between 54,000 and 67,000 tons in the last years of the 1860s. The Whitwood figures had increased first of all in the mid 1850s:-

	tons
1853	1,153
1854	3,660
1855	5,004
1856	13,100

At Briggs' Newton Colliery (H.K. Spark's from 1863), which had no railway connection, the tonnage remained between 15,000 and 29,000 until 1867, after which it dipped:

	tons
1867	15,652
1868	4,311
1869	7,405
1870	8,421

Newton's largest individual tonnages in the period 1851-1855 were to Hull, and the second largest markets were on the Navigation itself, at Goole, Snaith and Selby. Smaller quantities were sold on the Ure to Ripon, the Derwent to Malton, the Market Weighton Canal, both sides of the Humber, up the Trent, on the Ancholme, up the Hull (but not onto the Driffield Canal), and further afield to Grimsby, Louth, Boston, up the Welland (in one year only), and to Wisbech, King's Lynn, Norfolk, Suffolk, Essex, London and, in two of these years, Kent.

In March 1854 a new agreement was reached between Henry Briggs & Son (the elder son, H.C. or Harry Briggs had entered the partnership in 1849) and Henry Spark of Darlington, with whom the partners were to have continued, and sometimes painful, dealings over many years. Spark had already been selling the Company's coals, and he now undertook to purchase the whole of the produce of the Whitwood collieries except that which was sold directly by the firm itself to Castleford, Wheldon (doubtless specified on account of the ten flourishing limeworks there) or York, plus coal sold direct to carts at Whitwood and coals sold via the Great Northern Railway. This last line had opened up the West Riding coalfield to the rich London and South of England markets on the opening of its direct line from Askern, north of Doncaster (where connections were made by rail with the northern part of the coalfield) and London, in 1850. Under the 1854 agreement, Spark agreed to pay the following pit-top prices:-

	s	d	
best screened	8	0	per ton
seconds	6	8	
riddled slack	5	0	
unriddled slack	3	0	
seconds unscreened	5	8	

His selling prices were to be guided by the prices recommended by "the Leeds District and General Coal Masters Association" for so long as the Briggses remained members. He was to employ agents to encourage trade on the York & North Midland Railway (to become a part of the new North Eastern Railway in 1854), the Leeds Northern (also to join the new company), the Midland and in London. He was also to sell a minimum of 60,000 tons a year or pay 2d a ton on the deficiency, and he was to have the use of 60 hopper waggons - ie bottom-opening waggons, as used on the railways which became the North Eastern – and other railway waggons belonging to the Briggses, at a rental. The agreement was terminable after March 1st 1856 on six months' notice, but it apparently worked smoothly, as Spark was to join the Briggs' co-partnership himself in 1858.

One of the major advantages of the Whitwood Colliery site was its position close to a major junction of railways, radiating to each point of the compass. The coal shipping ports of Goole and Hull lay to the east and were also served by modern waterways. Rich agricultural markets served by rail and water lay to the north and the east, and heavy industry to the west and south. The Midland route, opened locally in 1840, had not been available for coal carriage from Yorkshire, but from 1850 there was a direct rail link with London and, in the mid-1850s, the Aire & Calder Navigation, having just decided to compete with the new railways, made special facilities available for the Company, in return for a specified minimum annual shipping tonnage. The Aire & Calder had through connections into the heavily-industrialised Calder valley above Wakefield and, via the Aire and the Leeds & Liverpool Canal, with the industrial towns of the Aire valley. It also had connections directly as far north west as Ripon and out into the valley of the Ouse and Humber and their tributary rivers and canals, and into the North Sea. In 1855 Briggs asked the Navigation for a riverside loading basin, and the Navigation responded with a request for an *'understanding'*. In the same year the Navigation was told that Briggs had got to the Stanley Main coal and now offered to ship a minimum of 30,000 tons a year for ten years, instead of the between 3000 and 5000 tons they were currently shipping. By the end of 1857, with the basin in use, the traffic was reported as being *"much above the guarantee"*. The Navigation had calculated that the basin would cost £1000, but the gain in freights would be over £900 a year. This was the first such basin, but others were built later, both for the Briggs' collieries and others. One reason for an increased interest in water carriage on the part of the Briggs' partners was over-production of coal by West Riding coalmasters using the Great Northern route to supply the South of England markets. In January 1855 William Aldam, the Navigation's chairman, noted the situation in his personal notebooks:

"G.N.R. Coal trade is now overdone - the stations are now everywhere glutted with Coal - which cannot be sold fast enough -"

By 1870 the Company was supplying coal by water as far upstream as Skipton (to Sidgwick & Company, who were large-scale cotton mill owners there), and they employed Thomas Murgatroyd, a Skipton coal agent, as their own agent, paying him a commission of 3d a ton. At Leeds, the partners bought a coal wharf for a substantial £3700. This wharf, of some 1730 square yards, with house, offices and two steam cranes, was leased to the new Company in 1869 for 14 years at £120 a year. Not all coal going to Leeds went through this yard, however, and in 1863 R.M. Carter, a Leeds coal merchant, cloth finisher and an alderman, who from 1868 until 1876 was also one of the MPs for that borough, owned some 20 coal boats and it cost him 1s 9d a ton, including lifting the coal from boat to cart, to carry between J. & J. Charlesworths' and Briggs' pits and his three wharfs in Leeds at the Calls, Victoria Bridge and Wellington Bridge. In 1863 he had been in the coal trade some 18 years and he sold about 30,000 tons of house coal a year. In 1869 a brickmaker from Woodhouse in Leeds owed the Company £29 4s 11d for coal supplied. To Leeds and on the whole of the Aire & Calder Navigation, the growing facilities of the railways were paralleled by the improvements made on and by the Navigation, especially in relation to the waterway's lock lengthening, its introduction of the compartment boat system, which was similar to a railway train on the water, and its use of hydraulic power for unloading purposes at its terminals. Numbers of independent boatmen survived, but did not always possess vessels in the best of conditions. For example, in 1884 a boat which was described as being old and leaky, sank at the Company's Methley staith while carrying 15 tons of best coal and 44 tons of seconds.

The Company also had a major business at Bradford by 1863, largely if not entirely carrying coal there by rail. In 1873 agreement was reached for the year-to-year tenancy of coal offices in Bradford at £52 a year and three firms of Bradford general carriers agreed to cart from each of the three major railway coal yards in the town, each for one year, as follows:-

J. & N. Taylor of Stones Street, from the Midland Coal Yard at 1s 8d ton first mile, 3 shillings for one to three miles

J. Parkinson & Sons, Harris St, Leeds Road, from GN Coal Yard at 1s 5d to 3 shillings.

Joseph Baldwin, Wigan St, from the L&Y Coal Yard at 1s 6d under one mile, 2 shillings one to two miles, etc.

The Guiseley & Yeadon Coal Co. Ltd was also supplied with coal by contract, and Thomas Murgatroyd of Skipton, already mentioned, was the Company's agent in Skipton, in the country to the north west of that town, and in the contract supply to the Barrow Haematite Steel & Iron Co. in Cumberland. In 1873 Murgatroyd ran 30 of his own waggons for the Company's coal on the Furness, Midland and LNW Railways' lines beyond Skipton.

Also in the Aire valley, the Company agreed to supply the coal required by the great firm of Sir Titus Salt and Company of Saltaire from April 1st 1874, via Fletcher and Eastby, a firm of Shipley coal merchants, at a commission of 4d a ton. This coal could have travelled by either rail or water. J.F. Easby had an extensive business in merchanting coal and lime at the Midland Railway stations at Bradford, Otley, Guiseley, Newlay and Kirkstall. He had 97 'A' shares and 246 'B' shares in the Company itself, plus 117 shares at £4 (all paid) in the Craven Lime Company and 235 shares in the Carlton Iron Company (the successor to Briggs' Cleveland Iron Company). This gave him strong connections with the Briggses and he was helped by the company when in financial difficulties. However, when he failed in 1883, the company put an agent into his house and business.

In 1873 business was opened with a firm of coal merchants in Hunslet, south Leeds, with the same surname as the Company's own bookkeeper at Whitwood, James Wild, and he became surety for the merchants in the sum of £400. Samuel Norris, a commission agent, became the Company's agent in Wakefield in 1874, and in the early 1870s the firm also had offices at Railway Street, York, from which sales were made, *inter alia* no doubt, to Scarborough. In the 1860s sales were made through the Norfolk & East Suffolk Coal Company which had depots at stations at Norwich, Great Yarmouth, etc. They took Briggs' Stanley Main coal at seven shillings a ton and (Northern Coalfield) Hartley's at 5s 9d. A coal merchant from Tuxford, Nottinghamshire, owed money in 1871 for Stanley Main or Whitwood Best coal received from the Company. Further south, in the early 1870s Jackson & Wood of Peckham Park Road, London, coal agents (sic), agreed to take 100 tons of Haigh Moor (ie best) coal at 6s 8d a ton, and in 1872 Frederick Warren Warren & Company, of Trumpington in Cambridgeshire and of 4 Great Eastern Railway Coal Depots, Whitechapel, Middlesex, became the Company's London agents for the year, being supplied with 150 to 200 tons a week, but having no concern with the Briggs' coal which was supplied to the Agricultural & Horticultural Association of 35 King Street, Westminster. The 1875 London trade directory shews that the Briggses had then no direct representation in London. The situation of the Briggses in Hull is not reflected in the surviving documentation, suggesting that perhaps little Briggs' coal was sold there, but at Goole their business was a quite major one.

One of the obvious practical difficulties facing the firm during the period of shortage of ready capital for new works was that of financing the provision of coal waggons with which to get the coal to markets. The railways only provided waggons in a small number of cases and so the vast majority of waggons had to be provided by the coal merchants or by the colliery concerns themselves. To obviate the difficulties caused by large amounts of capital being tied up in waggon ownership on the collieries' part, railway waggon hiring firms were established, and two of these - the Wakefield Rolling Stock Co. Ltd and the Yorkshire Railway Waggon Co.

Ltd - were centred on Wakefield. Another was formed at Barnsley in 1876 to take over the waggon works there which were run by G.W. and T. Craik, who were also the owners of the East Gawber Hall Colliery.

The Wakefield Rolling Stock Company was registered in November 1872 with a capital of £150,000, but the Yorkshire Company was the one favoured by the Briggs' company, Henry Briggs having subscribed for shares on its promotion in 1863. The capital was to be £30,000 in £10 shares, and the company was to purchase, repair, make and lend waggons. Two of the other major shareholders were William Teall, the Wakefield grease manufacturer and ironfounder, and Edward Green, the Wakefield economiser-builder and ironfounder. Henry Briggs bought 25 shares. He was one of the first directors and was still on the board in 1868, the year of his death. The company was soon successful, paying a 20% dividend for the year 1867. However, the Briggs' company did not apparently take advantage of the availability of locomotives for hire, but instead purchased their own engines from 1861, being among the first West Riding colliery owners to do so. Four engines were purchased in the first decade of their locomotive ownership and their names were *Comte de Paris* and *Elcho* (both names from visitors to the collieries), *Co-operator* and *Emperor of Brazil*. The colliery rules of 1856 had in fact provided for locomotive engine men, but it is not known whether there were any at that time or not. When the Wakefield Company sold out to the Yorkshire Company in 1892 for £43,675 18s 7d, it possessed 1542 waggons and one locomotive.

By agreement with various waggon companies and individual owners, Briggs took 259 waggons between April 1859 and November 1864, on leases of three, seven (a majority) and ten years. Ten were specified as carrying seven tons, but the capacity of the remainder was not stated. Most were side-emptying and only 10 had bottom doors, the type which was necessary for working on the North Eastern Railway's extensive system. The rents of most were between £10 and £12 12s 0d a year, but one lot of fifty was rented at £22 per waggon per year. The number of waggons in the leased lots varied between one and fifty-five, and the heavy capital expenditure by the Company, though spread over a period of years, totalled very nearly £17,000. Twenty-two waggons were also bought outright. These were all flat ones with side doors, ten of which could carry seven tons each. To buy outright, the cost was just over £50 each. The cost of hiring varied according to type, as follows:-

flat, with side doors	£10 to £11		
hoppers, with bottom doors	£11	10s	0d
flat with side and bottom doors	£10	10s	0d

The only exception was in the case of the fifty flat waggons with side doors which were hired at £22 each in 1861, but only for a three year period. A typical hiring, of twenty hopper waggons at £11 10s 0d each for seven years from May 1859 cost a total rental of £1610, whereas they would have cost above £1100 to purchase outright.

From the end of 1866 to the beginning of 1869, agreements were reached for a further 361 waggons, the majority leased from the Yorkshire Railway Waggon Co in batches of up to 80 and for periods of between 4¼ and seven years, although most were taken for seven years. It seems that Briggs' building of their own waggon shed in 1870s marked the beginning of their independence from the waggon leasing companies, and by 1892 and 1894 neither the Wakefield nor Yorkshire companies, respectively, had waggons which were leased to the Briggses.

As bright, washed coals became more and more desirable in the markets, small coal was necessarily produced in larger quantities from that source, and of course it also came from the breakage of larger coal in transit both above and below ground. Small coal was sold for as little as sixpence a ton, and much was used as railway ballast. A coking plant was being considered in May 1882, when overtures had been received from a firm which wished to erect such a plant at Whitwood on a piece of land which it proposed to take on a 21 year lease from the surface owner, with access to the railways and to the Navigation. The promoters wished to supply by-product gas for the firing of the Briggs' colliery boilers, but Lord Mexborough's agent was discouraging.

However, the idea was sown, and in 1883 a new company, The Whitwood Chemical Co. Ltd, was registered with a capital of £60,000 and the foundation stone of the works was laid in January 1884. The firm of Briggs took £10,000 in shares, with individual members of the firm taking further shares. The contractors were Robert Dempster & Sons of Elland, a firm specialising in gas plant manufacture and in chemical and hydraulic engineering work, which had been established in 1855 and which also took a share in the business. The works were opened in August 1884 and, after a short period of closure in 1885, were re-opened in the September of that year, becoming highly successful as "*much coke was shipped to Scandinavia, whilst German dye works took much of the benzol.*" The Chemical Works survived until the 1930s and the buildings until the 1960s. At Snydale Colliery, the Briggses owned and worked the normal coke ovens.

Gas was made at Whitwood from 1869 from a portion of the small coal produced there. The Briggses owned the gas-making plant and from it supplied not only their own works - their roadways, workshops and stables, presumably underground, being described as "*well and abundantly lighted*" - but also a number of residents in both Whitwood and Normanton townships, while at the request of the Whitwood Local Board, established in 1867, they laid mains and provided public lighting. In the adjoining Normanton township, negotiations were in hand in 1878 for the public supply of the Normanton area, even though a gas (and nominally water, too) company had supplied Normanton town from October 1870, as Briggs' gas was cheaper than that supplied by the other company. In 1878 Parliamentary Bills were promoted by the Whitwood and the Castleford Local Boards and by the Normanton Gas Company, all seeking powers to supply Whitwood with gas. When the Briggses petitioned against the schemes, the Whitwood and lower Normanton areas were withdrawn from the proposals. It was urged on the Briggses' part that, although to date profits had been but small, their gas undertaking was now "*becoming prosperous*".

However, in due course the gasworks were divorced from the colliery undertaking. In 1850 a Castleford Gas Light Company had been provisionally registered and it issued a prospectus in January 1851, referring *inter alia* to the benefits of "*the production of Artificial Light of greater illuminating power, and at a cheaper rate*". It was probably in 1873 that this company was bought out by the new Castleford & Whitwood Gas Light & Coke Co. Ltd, with a capital of £11,000, and that company obtained its own Act in 1878, although opposed by a rival Bill promoted by the Castleford Local Board. During the excitement over rival promotions, the agent of the Castleford and Whitwood Company was convicted by the magistrates for intimidation and corruption. The community of Whitwood Mere, incidentally, was provided with gas from Mitchell Brothers' glassworks plant. At Whitwood Collieries, the Silkstone seam was of excellent quality for gas making.

Although the partners had powers under various of their leases to produce bricks, it seems unlikely that brickworks for other than internal consumption were envisaged before the late 1860s. But the enormous boom in building, and especially in house-building in brick, led the Company to establish its own major brickworks close to the great new coal-winning at Loscoe Grange. Here in August 1869 a lease of a bed of clay was taken as from October 1869 for 21 years, and in 1870 a licence was purchased to use an improved form of kiln for burning bricks etc (sic) at Loscoe, from the patentees Messrs Wedekind, Craven & Chamberlain. Craven was the John Craven of Bradley & Craven of Wakefield, engine builders and clayworking machinery makers, while Humphrey Chamberlain, MIME, was an agent and manufacturer, and Hermand Wedekind was from London. In 1874 they took out a joint patent for kiln improvements. It had been suggested in 1870 that the Company should establish a Loscoe Brick & Tile Company, as a limited company, but Archibald Briggs decided to abandon that prospect and to manufacture directly through his own company. At the demolition of the great waggon repair shed at Whitwood in 1990, it was found to have been built of bricks with the initials 'HB W', which stood for Henry Briggs, Whitwood.

HOUSING AND SOCIAL ACTIVITITY

The practice of building cottages for workpeople wherever land offered had been adopted by the partners in the 1850s and 1860s. For example, 12 cottages were built on one plot and 15 on another, some distance away, with both groups lying well away from any other houses.

A major difficulty in direct house building lay in the large amount of capital tied up for many years by that process. But a method of controlling a part of the housing stock which was needed by the Company, and without major investment in it on their part, was used before incorporation in 1865 as, in February 1864, Henry & H.C. Briggs had taken a lease of 24 houses at Whitwood, owned by Amos Cheesbrough, a Castleford shopkeeper. They owned other houses by purchase, as in the case of the village of Methley Junction, where, to judge from the longevity of the houses, a better quality of dwelling existed.

Something is known of one of the developments which provided housing for Briggs' workers via a system of leasing back cottages to the Company. This concerns the village built in the years 1873-4 with the name of Loscoe Grove, an ancient local name, incidentally, and not one derived from the Loscoe in Derbyshire, from which numbers of men came to work in this area. The site was conveyed to the Company in 1872 and then sold off to investors. The majority (at least) of the houses were built by Richard Tadman, who bought some 2½ acres at Loscoe from the Company in June 1872 for £939 5s 0d. He was a newly-established builder and contractor in Thornes Lane, Wakefield, where Tadman Street was to perpetuate his name, and for some years his building business and his Calder Steam Sawing, Planing & Moulding Mills flourished, although he got into financial difficulties in 1879. The scheme was comprised of 113 cottages, in eight rows, six of which were back to backs and the other two runs of 34 through and larger cottages, and upon completion the houses and the land on which they lay were conveyed to investor owners. For example, in March 1873 Tadman had received a deposit of £200 on £2530 for 22 houses at Loscoe from Mrs H.M. Simon of 3 Headingley Terrace, Leeds, the houses being "*now in the course of erection*", with the balance to be paid upon completion. Most of the houses were financed by their purchasers' taking out mortgages, and the occupations of the investors is interesting - a Darton mining engineer, a Whitwood miner, a Wakefield printer, a Normanton railway station agent, a Darton bookkeeper (no mortgage), a Dewsbury innkeeper, a Loscoe Grove shopkeeper, and a Wakefield boot and shoe dealer. Nine houses here at Loscoe Grove were leased by the Company for 21 years from 1874 from the Rev James Cleave, a United Methodist Free Church minister, who also owned houses at Streethouse, a nearby mining community, in 1873.

As the Loscoe Grove cottages were completed in 1873 and 1874, their owners let them in batches to the Company, which paid rents of between £8 and £22 per house, and of course they were sub-let by the Company to tenants.

At Normanton Common, adjoining the Loscoe development, the Briggses also leased back houses from their speculative owners, and in this instance papers survive which illustrate the leasing back arrangement. During the months of April to September 1875, the Company leased 69 cottages from their owners, all for 21 years, all at Normanton Common and all subject to the Company's payment of rent, repairs and rates. The Company also had to paint the inside woodwork with two coats of oil paint, and agree to the three-yearly white-washing or colouring of the cottages internally, and also paint the exterior woodwork every three years. The cottages also had to be insured against fire. For example, 16 cottages were rented at £179, with all rents payable quarterly to the lessors, and insured for a minimum of £2000.

The lessors were:

	Cottages	Rent		
		£	s	d
Edwin Foster, Manningham, cashier	16	179	0	0
Thomas Sterland, Loscoe Grove, bookkeeper, and his mortgagees*	5	56	0	0
Joseph Bradley, Bolton in Lancashire, mechanic, ditto	16	179	0	0
William Bywater, Whitwood, foreman joiner, ditto	6	67	4	0
Young Womack, Chapel Row, Normanton, waggon builder, ditto	5	56	0	0
James Ingham, Whitwood accountant	21	268	16	0

* - all the mortgagees were with the Wakefield & West Riding Permanent Benefit Building & Investment Society.

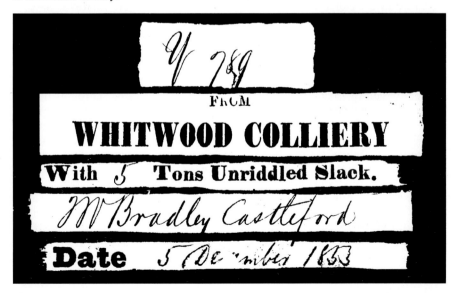

Fig.13 Coal waggon label used in 1853.

Of these, Ingham was a senior Briggs' employee, Ste(i)rland, one of the Company's clerks, had been the first clerk and collector to the Normanton Local Board, and Young Womack may have worked for them. His was an interesting story, as he was born in about 1833 into a boat-building family, then located on the Barnsley Canal at Agbrigg near Wakefield and later also at a boatyard at Stanley Ferry. Large numbers of wooden vessels had been built there until Young and his father Samuel failed in 1859, but Young Womack remained in the business of forming containers for the carriage of coal, although those now ran upon wheels rather than upon waterways.

At Streethouse (Whitwell Main) Colliery, the Briggses leased 24 cottages in July 1875 from their owner, Miss F.R. Ellison of Wakefield, adjoining the site of the proposed Congregational Chapel, the building of which still stands. The rent was to be £302 12s 0½d for 21 years from November 1st 1874, with the lessees being responsible for maintaining the houses and the owner having to insure them for at least £2500.

As early as August 1853, H.C. Briggs had bought land at Whitwood - probably that surrounding the site of the present Mexborough Arms - for £92 6s 6d. In November 1853, when he mortgaged the property to the Provincial Benefit Building Society of which he was a member, he borrowed £660 in respect of his eleven shares. The property consisted of 2462 square yards of land and twelve houses in course of erection. The Company also built some houses themselves at Normanton Common, on land which they had bought in 1864. By 1873, when the partners sold the property to the Company for £1170, there were some 7¾ acres of land and two long rows, probably of 43 and 42 houses and their outbuildings, respectively forming Foxbridge Row and Chapel Row, with one row containing 16 back-to-backs.

In these new villages, nonconformity existed and, to some degree, flourished. By 1865 Providence Chapel had been built at Normanton Common by the United Methodist Free Churches, in their Wakefield Circuit, when the site was conveyed to trustees on behalf of that denomination. Three of the six of these were Normanton Common miners, and another a blacksmith of that place. The land was sold at one shilling per yard, 345 square yards in all. In 1870 a draft was prepared for a conveyance of a site to the Primitive Methodist trustees and their Pontefract Circuit Superintendent Minister, for £34 2s 3d, where five of the 14 trustees were Normanton colliers and two others Normanton men, a tailor and a labourer. The remainder were of Altofts (two), Castleford (four) and Whitwood Mere. In this deed, the only Briggs' interest was that of their reversionary interest in the site. The Briggs family members' own concern with missioning in the area on the part of the rational dissenters, the Unitarians, came to nothing at all. In 1854, Henry Briggs and his son, H.C. Briggs, who was treasurer of the West Riding Tract and Village Mission Society, offered that society £20 per year towards the cost of a second missionary if the mission would include the Castleford and Whitwood areas within his area. The Briggs' offer was renewed in 1857 and Thomas Todd of Dewsbury offered a further £10. At Methley Junction, a Primitive Methodists' chapel site was bought from the Company in June 1875 for £35, the conveyance being to a grocer, eight miners, a blacksmith and an engine tenter, all of Methley Junction, and a collier of Methley Common. The chapel site stood within the hollow square of the colliery village of Methley Junction, and the 'Prims' were of the Leeds 4th Circuit.

The actual cost of building houses varied considerably. Thirty-eight houses, in blocks of one, two (for each of three owners, one of whom owned four houses), three (four owners), four (three owners) and five (one owner), cost between £67 and £222 10s 0d per house, and they were built by six separate builders. Three houses, which were built by Wright & Cook for Joseph Dean, cost the following:-

	£	s	d
Land	22	4	0
Brick	60	0	0
Lime	10	?	?
Sand	5	3	0
Laths	2	5	0
Slating	14	0	0
Bricklayer	45	0	0
Joiner	56	0	0
Fixtures	19	0	0
Stone	22	0	0
Digging	1	0	0
Boundary wall	3	10	0

John Pickles, who was a colliery storekeeper for the Briggses and was to become chairman of the Normanton School Board, owned property, probably his own house, Foxbridge Cottage, and another, at Foxbridge and Normanton Common, built between July and October 1866 at a cost of £350, of which £294 14s 9d was borrowed from the Briggses and paid off from rents in instalments between 1866 and 1873. After the first year, these houses returned between £5 15s 11d and £7 16s 9¾d per year, after paying interests, rent, rates and repairs, up to and including 1893. More cottages were built, apparently for Pickles and at nearby Beckbridge, between March and August 1875, at a total cost of £2200. These were less regularly let, and from 1877 to 1881 the rents and returns were low, with the return varying between £0 12s 11d and £6 18s 10¾d between 1875 and 1893. Pickles built his own new home, Hawe Villa, nearer to the centre of Normanton and in a somewhat more socially acceptable neighbourhood, between March and June 1887 at a cost of £295. He also bought six 'A' shares and five 'B' shares in the Company and sold them to a Bradford engineer for £194 in 1875.

H. Burnley, for some years a member of the Normanton Local Board and himself a master builder, invested heavily in such housing, ultimately possessing:-

		£	s	d
20 houses in Walker's Field, gross rental		195	0	0
Butcher's shop and house at Loscoe, net rental		19	10	0
2 shops near co-op	"	36	8	0
2 six-roomed houses adjoining last	"	28	12	0
2 shops with five-roomed house, adj	"	39	0	0
9 double houses, Co-op Field	"	109	4	0
12 " " Mill Lane	"	139	0	0
10 " " Mill Lane	"	123	10	0
16 six-roomed houses, Oxford Street	"	208	0	0
9 double houses, Good Hope Place	"	128	8	0
Hope Cottage and office	"	20	0	0

The growth of the colliery and the development of what was initially a dispersed colliery community led eventually to the establishment of a church at Whitwood, which was one of three townships within the ancient ecclesiastical parish of Featherstone, although in fact Castleford church lay rather nearer to Whitwood village and closely adjoining to Whitwood Mere. In 1865 a church was erected by public subscription at Whitwood and dedicated to St Philip. A site was given by the new Earl of Mexborough, the local major land (and coal) owner, and the subscription list was headed

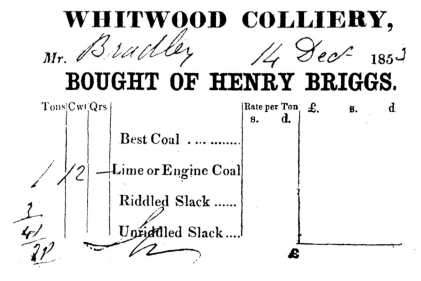

Fig.14 A coal account of 1853.

by Lord Mexborough. The Incorporated and the Ripon Diocesan Church Building societies each subscribed £200. George Pearson, the Pontefract railway contractor who was a partner in the firm of Pope & Pearson, colliery owners of nearby Altofts, gave £50, as did the Leeds banker John Calverley of not-very-distant Oulton Hall. The Briggses gave £40, and other subscriptions, in amounts from £25 downwards, came from country landed gentlemen, men of commerce and banking, professional men and ecclesiastics. The new church seated 320 and was built in the approved Early Decorated style. Another interesting contributor (of £25) was the Reverend Dr Pusey, the great Victorian high churchman and Regius Professor of Hebrew at Oxford. When he died in 1882, at the age of 82, his death was mentioned in the local church magazine. He also took an active part in obtaining the endowment of the living with £170 a year by the Dean and Chapter of Christ Church, Oxford, owners of the great tithes. As a result, the incumbent of the church, the Reverend J.A. Armitage, MA, was the Rector of Whitwood and he also gave £25 to the church building fund.

The architect was Joseph Clarke, FSA, of London, and the cost was some £3000. As built, the church had no tower, on grounds of cost, but one was added in 1870 as a public memorial to Henry Briggs, who was of course ecclesiastically a Unitarian, by subscription by *"friends, agents and workpeople"* of the colliery. The spire which is shewn surmounting this tower in the parish magazine in 1882 and 1883, was apparently never built. A publicly-funded monument to the memory of H.C. Briggs, also a Unitarian, was also erected in the graveyard of Whitwood church, in 1882.

A Wesleyan chapel was also built in Whitwood village, and this still stands, although now used for lay purposes. Its congregation's register of baptisms begins in 1858 and a chapel is referred to in the directory of 1861, but not that of 1857. The building was licensed for marriages in March 1873 and the chapel closed in 1960 or 1961.

As the collieries developed, so the population grew and the need for public services developed. In most of the townships in which the Briggs' collieries were significant employers of labour, there were also other employers whose presence, as reflected in the total population figures, makes an overall assessment of the Briggs' contribution in this field difficult. For example, in Normanton township employment was provided by three railway companies and by at least one other colliery concern, while in Whitwood the potteries and glassworks at Whitwood Mere complicate the matter. Probably only in Methley, which in any event had already a relatively high population, some part of which was concerned in coalmining long before the appearance of the Briggs' empire, can increases from 1861 be claimed to be almost entirely occasioned by Briggs' developments. However, the following tables may usefully serve to demonstrate the overall pattern:

1. Population.	Methley	Normanton	Whitwood
1801	1234	276	233
1841	1702	481	417
1851	1926	495	576
1861	2472	563	1723
1871	3277	3448	3342
1881	4074	8038	4102
1891	4357	10234	4806
1901	4271	12352	4873

2. Rateable value.	Methley £	Normanton £	Whitwood £
1838	6625	1693	1601
1867	16296	3992	9005
1902	36723	42689[1904]	20881

Sanitary improvements came to Whitwood as a result of the formation of a Local Board in 1867, under the provisions of the Local Government Act of 1858. Although the firm's name was conspicuous only by its absence from the list of requisitionists for the formation meeting, the system of multiple votes used in the election of Local Boards enabled the firm to have a strong voice in local government, and in 1872 the firm's solicitors were consulted as to the eligibility of one of their employees to be elected as their representative (sic) on the Whitwood Board. In Normanton a Local Board was formed in 1872 and one of Briggs' clerks, Thomas Stirland, was appointed part-time clerk and rate collector to the new body in that same year. Perhaps the Briggs' interest in the Whitwood Board helped in the remedying of the situation of 1871 when one of the Board's own members claimed that it had *"never done anything"*. In 1886 it was reported that four members of the Normanton Local Board, with the chairman, represented colliery interests. In 1885 Briggs' cashier, G.H. Schofield, had been chairman of the Normanton Local Board.

Old Henry Briggs had been interested in developing co-operative retailing, and had chaired the 1867 public meeting which decided to form the Wakefield Industrial Co-operative Society. With his firm's major interest in the principle of co-operation, it was natural that H.C. Briggs should take an interest in co-operation, along with his brother, and this was certainly the case. The more advanced of the local coal masters, those who owned colliery villages, were involved with their workmen in the establishment of co-operative shops. These included Pope & Pearson at Altofts in 1867 and the Sharlston Coal Co. at New Sharlston in 1872. Archibald Briggs was chairman of the newly-established Normanton Society in 1871 and a Whitwood Co-operative Society was in existence in May 1874. A society, which may be the same, is referred to as the Hopetown and Whitwood society in an 1887 directory. In 1885 the receipts of the Altofts and Normanton Society were £2153, while those of Hopetown and Whitwood were £4838.

We may glance back a few years in another connection, that of education. While still an active partner in the Flockton Colliery, Henry Briggs had become closely and personally involved in educational matters, and several pages of the famous (or infamous) report of 1842 on the employment of women and children in mines were devoted to the nationally unique social and educational system at Flockton, which, the report claims, totally disproved "*the asserted inaccessibility of the poor to kindly and civilizing influences: and equally so to the doctrine that refinements and labour are incompatible*". Briggs himself, with the aid of a grant from the British and Foreign School Society, which was the Nonconformists' education society, had built a school at Overton, the village in which he lived and close to which were the Emroyd pits of the family business, around 1841, and in this school he himself taught on Sundays. The building, in a mock Tudor style, stood until 1976. Educational facilities were in due course provided at Whitwood, especially following the growth in the number of employees in the 1850s, and in the colliery byelaws of 1857 provision was made for all fines payable by the workmen to become a fund for "*a school now in contemplation & intended to be shortly erected*" both for the colliers' children and the pit-boys. In December 1860 the firm wrote that "*We have lately erected two School-rooms, each 30 ft x 20 ft, in the vicinity of our Whitwood Colliery, for the education of the children of our workpeople*", and a master had been engaged from Ashover in Derbyshire. There had been no school in Whitwood in 1839, but, as the population grew both in Whitwood village and in the Castleford suburb of Whitwood Mere, a school board for the township of Whitwood was established in 1877. It met for the first time in the March of that year and H.C. Briggs was appointed chairman. In December 1881 his son, Arthur Currer Briggs (then of Woodland House, Newton Road, Leeds) succeeded him as a member, and was such for several years. The firm continued to run its own school at Whitwood itself until 1886, when it was decided to close the school after the next examinations and to offer the tenancy of the buildings to the school board. The school then consisted of a mixed and an infants' school, with a schoolmaster's house. There were four teachers and two monitresses. The school board agreed to pay £55 a year as rent, while allowing the Whitwood Improvement Society and the Sunday School to continue to use the buildings. The school continued in public education authority hands for many years, and there is an excellent report upon its then condition in the West Riding County Architect's reports on school premises of c.1904. Subsequent to the County Council's building of a new school, one of the two school buildings was let for various (latterly Union) purposes, and was ultimately demolished in 1971. These curious little school buildings at Whitwood, built in (an adapted) Tudor style, retained until demolition the diamond-paned windows which had been condemned by the County Architect many years earlier when he said, "*The lattice windows are unsatisfactory, larger panes ought to be substituted*". A company report of 1867 refers to the recent building of a new infants' school - probably that which survived until 1971 - by the firm at a cost of £360. In a wider educational field, apart from his interests in the Wakefield

Mechanics' Institution and in his personal superintendency of the Westgate Chapel Sunday School, in 1857 Henry Briggs was one of the six committee members of the West Yorkshire Northern Association *"for awarding Prizes to the Children of Persons employed in Coal and Ironstone Mines"*.

Members of the Briggs family, and the firm itself, were major supporters of the Yorkshire College of Science, the predecessor of the University of Leeds of 1904. At its establishment in 1873, Archibald Briggs subscribed £25, his brother Harry became a Life Governor, and the firm subscribed £250. The firm was also generous to Leeds Infirmary, donating £100 in 1874 and giving a ten guinea subscription. Both Mrs (Henry?) and Mrs H.C. Briggs (then of Belvedere House, Harrogate) were members of the Yorkshire Ladies' Council of Education in 1880, though not on its committee. In 1869 the Company gained a prize medal at the Amsterdam Exhibition and for several decades used an engraved representation of it on their letter heads.

In addition to the more formal educational activities aimed at children, adult education and social intercourse were much encouraged by the firm and by individual members of the Briggs family. By 1882 there was a Briggs-built Reading Room at Hopetown, Normanton Common. Mrs Briggs hoped to establish other such reading rooms at Whitwood and Methley, and it was then intended to add cocoa taverns to each of these, in which the workmen might take shares. It was hoped that these would be in themselves *"as attractive as possible"*. In the following year, 1883, a reference is made to a concert given in Briggs' carpenters' shop in aid of the Streethouse Colliery's Working Men's Reading Room and Library.

This is something of the story of the earlier growth of the great firm of Henry Briggs, Son & Co. Ltd, which survived until Nationalisation in 1947. Its story can be told in some detail largely on account of the survival in local solicitors' collections of the earlier papers of the concern, providing in many instances information of a kind which has usually not survived. It is a significant story.

The papers from which the information has been derived are now all in The John Goodchild Collection, Local History Study Centre, below Central Library, Drury Lane, Wakefield, WF1 2DT. Where other sources have been quoted, they too are in the same Collection in original or copy form, as are the illustrations used here - and many others.